Stained Glass

Vital Peeters

The Art of Crafts

D1265596

First published in 1999 by
The Crowood Press Ltd
Ramsbury, Marlborough
Wiltshire SN8 2HR

British Library Cataloguing in Publication Data

A catalogue record for this book is available from the British Library.

ISBN 1 86126 299 X

Dedication
For Julian

Photographic Acknowledgements
Pages 10 and 11 (upper): photographs © Woodmansterne.
Pages 6, 9 and 11 (lower): photographs by Peter Smith of Newbery
Smith Photography.
Photographs on the above mentioned pages, by kind permission of the Dean
and Canons of Christ Church Cathedral, Oxford.
Pages 44, 52, 60, 64, 68 and 72: photographs by Foundry Design.

Typeset by D & N Publishing
Membury Business Park, Lambourn Woodlands
Hungerford, Berkshire.

Printed and bound by Leo Book Products, China.

Contents

Introduction

The art of stained glass has been with us since AD 400, whilst the earliest evidence of glass painting dates from AD 900. It was the Romans who invented the first glass windows ever recorded: these early windows consisted of small cast green glass slabs in wooden frames whilst, slightly later, it was probably the Byzantines who invented the lead to mount smaller pieces of glass together.

The first book on stained glass was written in the twelfth century by Theophilus, a German Benedictine monk, and there have been many books written on the subject since. The basic techniques are the same today as they were then so, why yet another book? You may well ask.

The twentieth century has seen renewed interest and a new approach to the art of stained glass. Not only has the medium become more widely spread outside places of worship, but more people have been able to practise this ancient craft as materials have become more available and affordable.

Increasingly, great artists have also recognized this medium as a magnificent means of expression. In the Middle Ages only a few highly skilled makers were allowed to use this most expensive material for religious buildings and it was not until the nineteenth century that ordinary people could even afford simple clear glass for their houses.

The revolution in glass-making techniques has also affected the manufacture of coloured glass. Whereas expensive hand-made glass is still being produced as it was in the middle ages, machine-made glass has vastly increased the choice and decreased the price to the ordinary consumer, making it possible for more people to make stained glass for their own homes.

Bad workmanship and design have, however, lead to some poor results but, as long as you are prepared to spend a little extra time working out your ideas and using a little originality, this need not be the case.

Whether you have worked in different media, or indeed never practised any kind of art form, I hope that this book will be of use to you. The most essential requirement for a good start is to share a certain delight in the beauty of glass. It is a worthwhile journey, and one that I have enjoyed for the last ten years. I have slowly learned and then experimented with the various techniques, although I never made it my conscious professional choice: glass chose me to explore its many possibilities.

Most of all, I hope that, like me, you will find a continuous joy in the process and appreciation of this art.

Have fun.

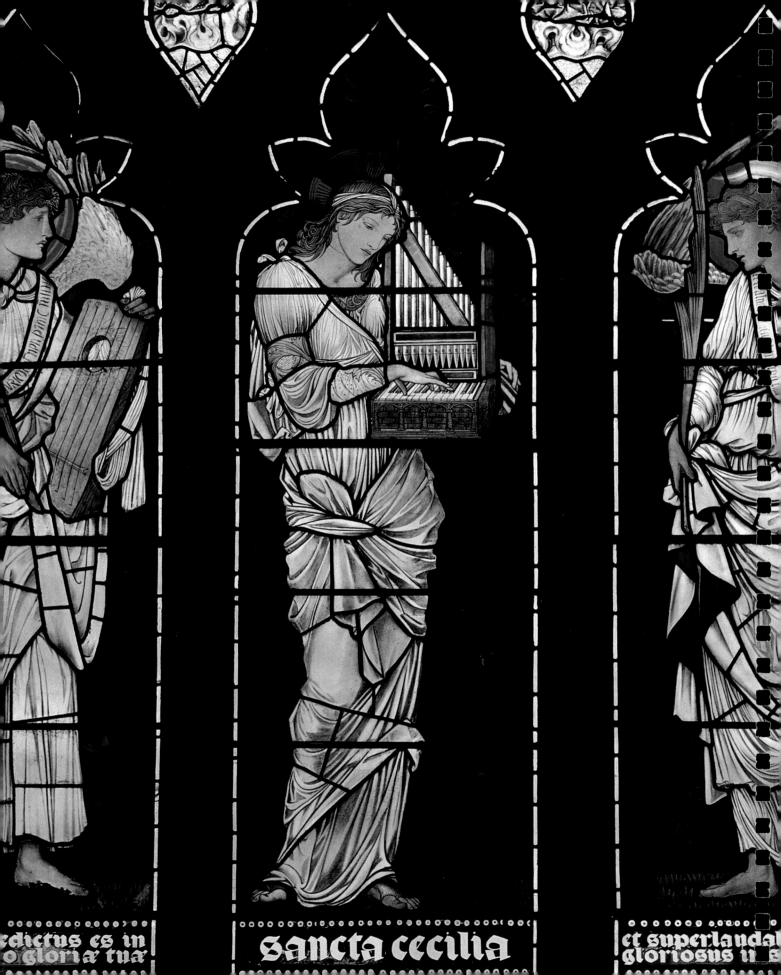

sanctacecilia

1 Looking at Stained Glass

WHERE TO LOOK

If you are lucky enough to live in a place with lots of stained glass windows in the vicinity, you can just take a walk and start exploring the local 'treasures'. *The Buildings of England* series, catalogued thoroughly by Nikolaus Pevsner, will guide you to historical sites where you can see examples of ancient glass in an architectural setting. If you do not live in England, check your local library or bookshop to find a guide to your area.

However, this is only a starting point; there are many good books specifically on the subject of stained glass, which will give you an insider's view of this fabulous medium.

Wherever you live you should start by going to look at some stained glass windows in a local church or chapel. Try looking at them with fresh eyes, better still, if you have a friend who is interested in the subject then ask them to accompany you – four eyes are better than two. If you are lucky, an organ playing in the background will help to set the mood.

HOW TO LOOK

Before you start, it is probably useful to disregard all the historical highbrow art texts you might have come across, to clear your mind and make you look creatively and critically. Try and decide what the glass does to you: does it make you feel uplifted, confused, moved, sad ...? If it speaks to you emotionally, stay with it, if not, move on to the next piece (you can always come back later to see if you have changed your opinion).

Now try and look beyond the window: how much light is coming through and how does the glass change the light and the interior that you are standing in? Is there movement in the composition of the window or is it very static? Does the glass appear flat or does it appear to tremble? Is the colour in the glass warm or cold, or both?

Now gently avert your eyes from this window and see if you can imagine the window without the stained glass. How would this change the mood and atmosphere of the space and architecture? Does the glass add anything?

INTERPRETATION

Your own reactions to these observations are important and it is best to build up the confidence to express your own personal opinions. This way you will discover and become intimate with your favourite

(Opposite) *The Morris windows, Christ Church Cathedral, Oxford.*

'views' in the world of stained glass. This does not mean adopting a clichéd 'I know what I like' attitude. To know what you like is to pick up a fleeting sensation and never bother to find out what it is that makes it special, which is rather like looking at pretty scenery when the real beauty is totally passing you by. Appreciating the subtleties of architectural and decorative glass is a learning process.

SEE THE LIGHT

What is the unique difference between looking at glass and any other form of art? The answer is *light*: in any other medium, light is reflected. If you think about it, shadows shape a sculpture, a light source bounces back onto a painting, a moving image is projected onto a static screen. Only with glass do you look directly at the light source. This is the fundamental character of glass and no other medium can so radically change the character of a space. Stained glass can flood a building in a magic, otherworldly light which automatically throws you into an alien environment. It forms a membrane which alters the quality of the daylight and, consequently, the view of the sky beyond. It has a strong psychological power over the way we perceive space.

If, however, you start looking critically at stained glass, there is still much more to its interpretation than simply its power to manipulate one's mood. The artist's ability to interpret the subject, select colours and textures of glass, or demonstrate his painting skills can be delights in themselves.

So how should you look creatively at this visual art? Take your time and let the work reveal itself to you. Ask your-self questions such as: 'Why is there so much red here?' or 'Why is the glass divided into squares instead of circular shapes?' and edit your observations; for example, you can choose to zoom in to a detail and look for its relevance in the complete composition or try and find out why blue is used in a particular window. But most of all …

BE CRITICAL

When somebody tells you that you should like all the windows in a certain cathedral or hall because they are important or highly praised by an expert, go and see them. They may be right but do not just accept their opinion.

There has been a lot of very mediocre work produced over the centuries and some of it is over-rated. A lot of glass made in the nineteenth century was too polished and over decorated, if not lifeless, and looks as if it has been ordered from pattern books and mass-produced by decorating firms. However, this is just my opinion and I hope that you will be critical and go and look for yourselves.

Of course I am biased towards certain styles and artists, however I can be persuaded to look at other work by an enthusiastic recommendation. You will be rewarded by keeping an open mind, but do not let it become polluted by trends and fads. It is undeniable that fashion, lifestyle and media will influence your tastes, but within those limits lie the real quality works as well as a lot of pale, bad imitations. There are also a lot of works in between, but aim high and always look for the best examples.

STILL CONFUSED?

For me it is always helpful to start with lots of questions; they make you think about the way looking at stained glass can help you form an opinion of the medium, without blindly following a guide book. In the following pages I will give a brief outline of the components of a glass window and analyse the aspects in a historical context. Lastly, the pleasure of absorbing the beauty and skill of stained glass is in actually making it and hopefully this book will help you to either learn or refine this skill.

ANALYSING HISTORICAL STAINED GLASS

You can see a great deal by studying photographs of stained glass windows but nothing beats looking at the real thing. To give you a taste of the creative masters of the past, I have chosen to show you some windows from Christ Church Cathedral in Oxford. This breathtaking glass is some of the best in the world and represents some of the finest of the last 600 years.

The Middle Ages are partly represented in this detail of the *Becket Window* (*see* right) which immediately throws you into an intriguing world of mad creatures and impasse. Could it be a medieval version of a vicious satirist or political cartoonist? The pure virtuosity of injecting these images into the stonework and the terrific sense of design and colour are masterly. We do not know who created the window, but this unknown master obviously had great control over the medium. In those days the artist would have been considered a skilled craftsman and have sufficient power to control the project.

The reason all medieval glass consists of smallish pieces is because the craftsmen did not possess the technology to make them any bigger. It was a hit and miss process as the glass was baked in holes in the ground on hot coals, which makes the delicacy of the pieces all the

The Becket window, Christ Church Cathedral, Oxford.

more surprising. The lead lines are creatively integrated into the designs and there is a great unity between the window structure and the glasswork.

The remarkable elegance and stylistic quality of this work is not naïve but equal to the sophistication of the classical style. I would even argue that a lot of the classical work produced in the sixteenth and seventeenth centuries is less sympathetic to the medium. Typically the method involved taking a lot of clear glass squares (by this time slightly larger

Windows from Christ Church Cathedral, Oxford: (right) *the Jonah window and* (opposite) *the Latin chapel East window.*

pieces of glass could be produced) and painting them in many different enamels. The impression you get from the classical work is of a giant painting on glass. The leadwork consists of a simple grid and is therefore purely functional, namely as a skeleton to hold the glass pieces together.

An exception is the *Jonah* window, which was made by Abraham Van Linge in 1631, where the pure quality of painting makes up for the shortcomings of the method used to produce it. See how the design continues through the two windows and how brilliantly the colours are selected and painted. However, when in later centuries some of the glass got broken and needed restoring, the cracks were less easily hidden and the replacement pieces applied by less skilled painters would often stick out like a sore thumb.

Victorian windows produced between the beginning and end of the nineteenth century make up the bulk of the windows to be seen in churches today. The new interest in church building, restoring and religious fervour has left us with large numbers of gothic-style windows, many of which were mass-produced and contain formulaic iconography. I find them often rather lifeless but they are extremely skilfully painted. There are notable exceptions, however, where the style and feel of the medieval windows are combined with the exceptional control and richness of colour of the nineteenth century window.

In the Latin chapel of Christ Church Cathedral, Oxford, the *East* window was designed by Burne-Jones in 1859 (*see* p.11). It tells the story of St. Frideswide, Oxford's patron saint. Unlike the *Jonah* window, this window is divided into many little scenes. It looks like a pattern from a distance, and does not 'read' until you get closer. However, the top roundel is more dramatic from this distance. Zoom into this and you can see a crowning piece showing St Frideswide

(*see* bottom p.11). The window has a sense of total design and clear direction of line and colour, and points the way forward to Burne-Jones's later development in the *Morris* windows from 1872.

The use of colour and the delicate painting style of the *Morris* windows is quite different from the earlier pieces and represents the last phase in our journey through the ages. This window shows a break with the past and the quiet meditative pose of the musician is more internal than any of the previous subjects. There is an obvious strong sense of colour, and the unusual green of the foliage seems to

enhance the depth in contrast to the light figure. It is also very stylistic in its minimal use of colour and is perhaps also closer to our aesthetic sense.

I hope that the few windows I have shown here give you a taste for exploring the different aspects of design, style and subject matter through the ages. Little has changed fundamentally in technical terms and, in fact, we still use the same basic ingredients today. However, there have been a number of exciting developments in stained glass since the Burne Jones windows were made and it is up to you to carry on the exploration and become inspired. Of course not all the work is as high in quality as the windows in this cathedral, but often it is the less successful work that is the most instructive and fun to analyse. So now let us leave the cathedral and move into the designer's studio.

2 Design Rules

Designing a stained glass window is like introducing a soul into your project: technique is important, but it is always the servant of the design! In the first part of this chapter, I will try and explain the particular ways of dealing with the design process. It is important to be sensible to the demands of the design and learn how to enjoy it, so I have compiled some rules which you may find helpful. You can then turn immediately to the next part of this chapter which deals with the practical guidelines, with some of my own work as examples. Do not accept them as necessarily the best way of achieving your goal – every individual has a different notion of what is a good or successful idea – but be assertive and open your mind to the wealth of possibilities.

THE BASIC RULES

Rule 1: You Can't Make Apple Pie with Pears

Look at your piece as a jigsaw, or a collage of different layers. Take any image and divide it up into blocks and draw a thick, black line between each block. All the lines should end up either in the frame or join another line, called the cut-line.

This line represents the position of the lead, the reason being that every shape

Image

Cut-line design

within your closed line will have to be cut out of glass. The shapes below are impossible to cut and you will need to round the sharp angles off and divide the long, narrow shapes up or make them wider. This means that the pieces of glass you cut will survive the process and general wear and tear.

As you can see, the shapes in the cut-line design are simplified to avoid complications. You will need to simplify the shapes, but find a satisfying way to do so. The tulip flowers are subdivided into three petals but will be united again by using the same, or similar, colour to suggest that it is the same bloom. There are

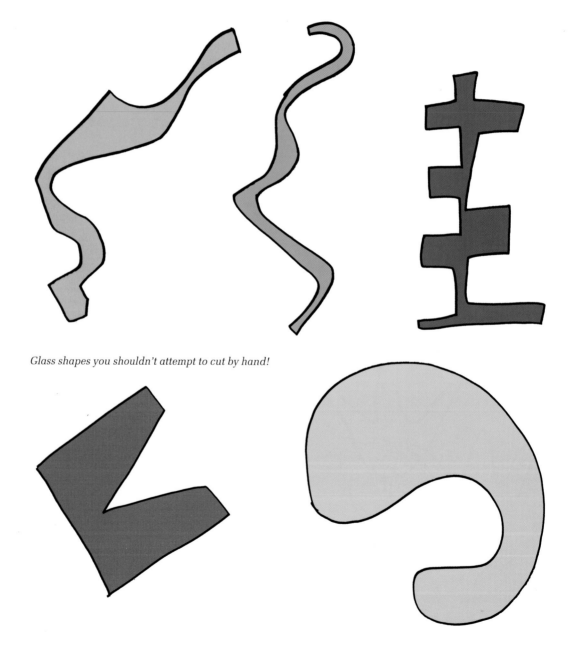

Glass shapes you shouldn't attempt to cut by hand!

many possibilities to compensate for the division of shapes in a manageable design, as you will see by studying the designs in this book.

Whether you are an experienced artist or an absolute beginner, the same rule applies for creating leaded glass panels. If you are a practising artist you might find the limitations of the form beneficial and discover a new direction to your design. It certainly had this effect on me as abstract art had not been part of my portfolio before I started using glass. It helped me to loosen up, stylize and simplify my ideas. For the person starting with no creative background, you can start with the simplest ideas and still end up with a satisfying design and your designs will become more sophisticated as you gain experience.

Rule 2: This Is No Brussels Lace

The essence of the medium is a frame with a well defined structure: the work is solid and quite heavy and the smaller it is, the clumsier it will look, so be bold, and remember that it has to be seen from a certain distance. Lead width can be from 3mm to 25mm, which is why you do not come across many pocket-sized panels.

Think space: windows, doors, architecture; the work is not a fresco, but more like a mosaic or, alternatively, more like batik than tapestry. It is usually site-specific, so if you can imagine the space where you want to put your glass, try and imagine how it will change the space. What is the quality of the light and how much light is there? Is it a meeting point or a quiet corner? If it is a meeting point, try to grab the attention by using bright colours or a wide, vigorous lead structure, and give it a big enough platform (you might start by having the builders in to make a bigger

opening in the wall). Obviously, an intimate corner does not need a grand theatrical gesture and, in this case, subtlety and detail are of greater importance.

It can be very useful to draw some lines on the window with a thick, water-based, felt-tip pen just to see the impact. You could also try to work out your design on as big a piece of paper as possible (or nearest to the real size, but make sure you draw it to scale, related to the real size). Although you are still at the early stages of your design, it is good to be aware of the size of the window and the position it can be viewed from, its function and the quality of the light. It is also a good idea to be aware of the budget, so that you can introduce more or less expensive glass depending on what you can afford (particularly important if you are tackling a larger project).

Rule 3: Sucking Your Pencil

It is entirely up to you if you want to copy a design or follow a rigid traditional pattern: Victorian lilies and thirties' sun patterns are readily available straight from the conveyor belt, flat packed and characterless; however, my feeling is that this would be a lost opportunity and I hope that you would like to go a little beyond predictable mediocrity.

Of course it is not going to be easy – no gain without pain – but I can offer you a few thoughts and encouraging hints. Firstly, choose an idea that is close to your heart, or persuade your commissioner to be flexible: it is so much more satisfying to bring some personal touches into your work. I usually get my best ideas while dog walking, sitting on a train, or chatting to a friend. The sudden flash of inspiration usually comes when you have been thinking subconsciously about your project for a while.

If, however, you are working to a deadline, you might get some good ideas by looking through magazines (I keep a whole pile of old favourites) or if you have a specific request, such as something reminiscent of the Renaissance, then look at relevant art books or take a sketch pad to a museum. If you have a particular subject or object to interpret, try compiling a picture bank (I made one by collecting and filing images from postcards, cuttings and leaflets).

You need to try and be aware that designing is an organic process: do not throw away all your thumbnails, doodles and sketches until you have scrutinized them, and perhaps copied some of the details that you like. Bear in mind that it can take minutes or weeks to finish something that you are happy with. Finally, if your head is hurting and you are going cross-eyed, then take a break; you will find that when you come back to the drawing board you will see your work in a different light. Be patient, a cathedral window was not made in a day.

Rule 4: Inspiration from Great Masters

Matisse and Chagall were two of the great masters whose paintings established them as brilliant artists, who then turned their attention to stained glass and looked at the medium in a totally fresh way. Chagall uses his black paint to blur the lead line and give the work a shimmering effect, whilst his use of flashed and stained glass washes the whole window in flurries of colour. Matisse on the other hand uses flat colour and sharp, structural lines, in luscious curves and straight grids, to reveal a startling simplicity.

Marc Chagall

Henri Matisse

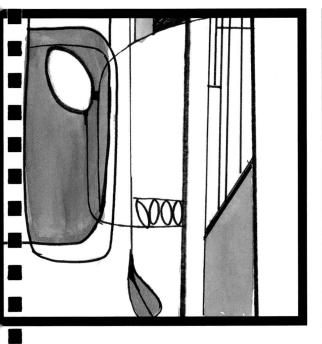

Charles Rennie Mackintosh

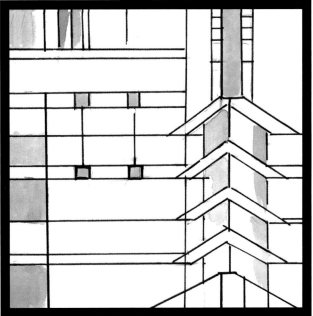

Frank Lloyd Wright

It is interesting to contrast these artists' work with architects Charles Rennie Mackintosh and Frank Lloyd Wright. Their use of colour is very minimal indeed; some soft pink opaques and a few lustres, but using strong, linear, symmetric designs. Their accent is on lead line and structure as an extension of their buildings. The illustrations show the style of each artist and demonstrate how different they are.

What these artists have in common, however, is their original approach and deep understanding of the medium. They manage to bring poetry and rhythm into the glass design and, when seen in the original form, to the fabric of the building.

What you need to bear in mind is that these artists produced the *designs*, not the windows themselves, and so behind each of these masters is another artist who interpreted their designs in stained glass. This is no mean feat but, sadly, this poor soul is often forgotten and remains nameless.

Rule 5: Composition Can Strike a Chord

Creating a successful stained glass panel is rather like an orchestra creating music. Whilst an orchestra works with a range of instruments, creating stained glass involves working with numerous textures, pure colours, layers of colour, different degrees of transparencies, stains and engravings; in other words a multi-layered range. Similarly the composition process involves working with rhythm, tonality and harmony, whilst the design process involves introducing movement, themes and rhythm. The effect of glass on people is also emotional and immediate like the way music touches the senses.

For example: if you want to achieve a feeling of summer in your piece, you

Power lines suggesting the nature of design.

Assertive

Restful

Soft–Organic–Intimate

Focused–Earthy–Excitement

Dynamic–Chaotic–Aggressive

Architectural–Rational–Geometric

should use warm glass colours. Similarly, it would be quite wrong to use sharp angles and geometric shapes to create a peaceful window. On page 18 are some examples of power-lines to suggest the nature of the design.

EXAMPLES

To illustrate this point here are a few examples of my work:

Texture

In this abstract window (*see* below), I used the texture of the glass to bring life to the window, I also used sandblasted glass to give luminosity and to create extra depth and dimension to the window. You can carefully choose the textures to contrast or complement each other. Frosting with an acid paste is another option (*see* Projects). As you can see from this example, texture can replace colour.

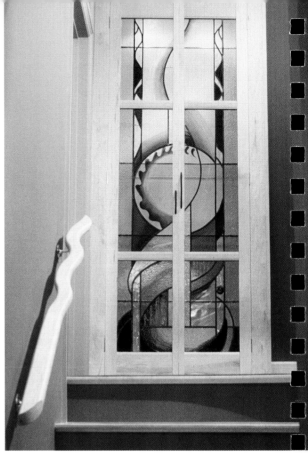

Colour

This is an example of interior work (*see* right). The glass in this china cupboard is backlit artificially and shows how the central motive picks out the colour of the walls. I also used a lot of clear glass so that objects displayed in it could be clearly seen.

Colours, or lack of them, can have a lot of power over a glass image. Select

colours carefully: two or three and their tones are usually more than enough. It is more striking if you can use less colour, interspersing with clear glass to bring the colour out more powerfully. Beware of red! It is a powerful colour and using lots of it could be blinding and confusing. Blue is a heavenly colour, particularly powerful in glass, and hence very popular; it is also very successful when combined with green and yellow. If you do choose to use more colours, try to use lighter tones as a mass of multiple strong colours can be an extreme assault on the senses. In order to be subtle you need a lot of confidence and a strong sense of direction.

Rhythm

This is a chapel window for a hospice (*see* left). I wanted to create a feeling of hope and peace. The wave-like and curvilinear lines are repeated throughout to compensate for the tall format of the window; the rhythm which is achieved in this way is calming and restful. The repeated circular shapes running vertically through the middle of the window create a feeling of movement, helped by the gradual lightening of colour towards the top. It is important to repeat certain motives and gradually change colour to create rhythm.

Mood

This rising star (*see* right) creates a mood of joy and optimism. The lead lines are deliberately free and unrestricted by rulers. The swirl in the middle enhances the mood of carefree abandon and the colours are bright and simple, almost

evoking a playground style. This example is quite straightforward and it is good to go back to basics at times but, obviously, you can also combine several moods to evoke, say, contrasting emotions.

Playfulness

In this kitchen window (*see* left), the idea of fruit and vegetables seemed appropriate. The freshness of lemon and cucumber are uplifting but also evoke, for me at least, the (very English) pleasures of gin and tonic or cucumber sandwiches on a hot summer's day.

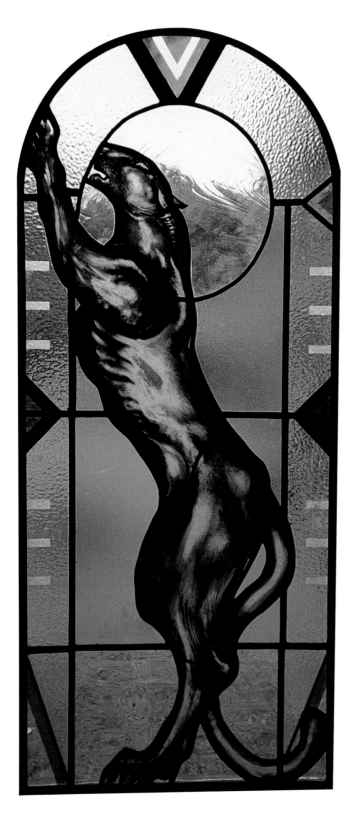

Drama

This ferocious panther (*see* left) guards the door to a sitting room and was commissioned for a house containing a beautiful painting of a panther. To create the drama, I painted it quite realistically. The plain background adds to the presence of the animal. It was based on an art deco design as this style is very dramatic.

Format

You do not need a rectangular shape as demonstrated by this piece (*see* opposite above) called *Sebastian*. This was made for an exhibition and therefore I could use a format to give it more drama. The triangle represents the aggressive, disturbing nature, whilst the circle represents passion and hope. The triangle has a double meaning: as an angular shape it is strong and rigid but it also has a symbolic meaning as it is combined with the colour pink – a symbol of the holocaust massacre and liberation of gay people. By using different shapes, or combined shapes, you can build up a picture which has multiple layers of meaning and is open to interpretation by leaving the clues deliberately vague.

Humour

There is passion in this picture (*see* opposite below) too, but of a different kind. The couple doing the tango are having a great time and, if you treat a subject light-heartedly, the tone changes significantly. Using parody, caricature and allusions is a great way to bring a smile to someone's face or to shock them into recognition. The medieval glass painters certainly are a good example, as illustrated in the previous chapter by the Becket window.

Linacre College window, Oxford.

Architectural Glass

This is the setting of the *Linacre College* window and demonstrates how the demands of architecture can play an important role in the design. Behind this window is a tall brick building with tall windows. To keep the visitors and students from looking straight into the rooms beyond, I used only textured glass. I also retained as much light as possible by using clear glass as the amount of daylight coming through the window was limited by the building behind it. The style is contemporary to reflect the interior, and with the strong diagonals from top right to bottom left I intended to reflect the direction of the staircase underneath the window.

Presentation

Once you have established your design, roughly coloured in your sketch and indicated the kinds of glass and textures you will be using, it is always a good idea to make a presentation of your design. Even if it is a small design for your own portfolio, it will help you to sharpen your ideas and refine the design.

Make sure that you have some idea of the thickness of the lead you want to use so that the impression of the final panel is as realistic as possible. Do not worry too much about the precise colours as some coloured glass might not be available.

It is also a good idea to work the design out to scale and to the size of the sheet of paper that you will be working on (if it is not life-size); this will help you to scale up the design to the real size later. I usually start by drawing the design in pencil: you might choose to draw it on a computer but, personally, I find this easier to do on paper as I always change some details when I scale the design up by hand.

The line drawing is then coloured in with water colours, as they give the most accurate impression of glass colours. However, you might prefer to work in pastels or colour pencils and you can certainly work on top of the water colours with those media. After the colouring process, I use felt-tip pens in various thicknesses to draw the lead-lines. Here then is an example of a design and the end product (*see* opposite).

If the process of designing has been an adventure, enabling you to open your eyes and explore new ideas, then it has been a success. If you also had a great deal of fun in the process, then it will have been a triumph. In my next chapter I will give you some tips on setting up your own workshop/studio and some advice about which basic materials and tools you will need.

Watercolour and felt-tip design on paper.

The finished glass panel.

3 Starting from Scratch

TOOLS

The first thing I would suggest is that you find a local stained glass supplier, using your telephone directory. The supplier should be able to give you the information you need, or order any specific tools or materials you might require. There is a bewildering array of tools on the market and catalogues will give you useful information about most of them; it is also fun to explore shops or warehouses when you are looking for new equipment. All I will do is describe the most basic equipment to start you off. You will build up an array of tools and materials as you get more familiar with the techniques and gradually build up your confidence.

BASIC TOOLS FOR CUTTING GLASS AND LEADING

Glass Cutters

Basic glass cutters are the tools used most frequently in the studio and are obviously essential to the work, but when you are starting out begin by using disposable cutters: they are cheap, work perfectly adequately and will help you to get to grips with the technique. However you should replace them after some use, or when you find that they do not cut smoothly any more, and then move on to using the more sophisticated glass cutters on the market. Each individual artist has different requirements, so do check that you can use the cutters offered by your supplier. You might also find it useful to book yourself into a stained glass class to practise your technique before you start work.

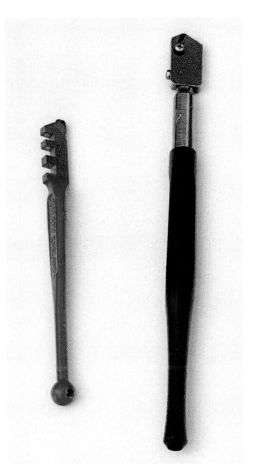

Glass cutters. The one on the left is disposable.

Grozing pliers.

Grozing Pliers

Grozing pliers allow you to 'nibble' the sharp edges and chips where the glass has been cut, thus preventing injuries; they also break off little sharp corners and refine the shape to fit.

Running Pliers

Running pliers help you to break the glass more easily; although they are not the most essential tool, I would recommend them as they are comfortable to use and help to speed up the work.

You will get the hang of using these tools fairly quickly, but do remember that it takes only a short time to become proficient but a long time to become a master. And who wants to be just proficient?

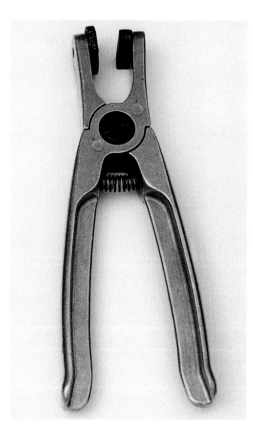

Running pliers.

Cutting a Piece of Glass

Step 1: Make sure the wheel of the glass cutter is well lubricated. I store mine in a jam jar with a spongy material in the bottom, soaked in cutting oil; this protects the wheel from wear and ensures that it cuts the glass smoothly.

Step 2: To cut a straight line into the glass, mark the position of your cutting line with a felt-tip pen, preferably black as this will show on any colour glass. Work on a white surface so that you can see the line, and use a ruler as this will help you to cut a more precise piece and make the following steps much easier.

Step 3: When scoring the glass, use a ruler to guide you in a straight line and hold it down tightly as the glass is slippery. Cut away from your body as this makes it easier to see the marked line;

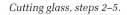

Cutting glass, steps 2–5.

the way you hold the cutter is irrelevant – whatever feels comfortable for you is the right position.

Step 4: When breaking glass using the running pliers make sure that the square rubber element on the top, and the middle mark on the rubber element, are both in line with the scoring line. You can also break glass with your hands, but this can be awkward if the piece is narrow, small or irregular in shape.

Step 5: If the cut edge of the glass has sharp splinters, you can groze it using the grozing pliers. These sharp edges are often the result of cutting curved lines and the best way of breaking the glass after scoring a curved line is to tap gently along the scoring line from one end to the other. It is important to tap on the side you are cutting away, using the heaviest side of the glass cutter and tapping at short intervals to avoid chipping the glass.

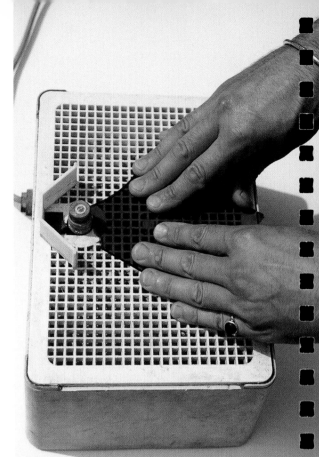

Glass Grinder

The next tool you will need is a glass grinder which is a versatile tool used for smoothing the rough edges of pieces of cut glass, or making complex shapes; it is also a fast way of ensuring that your pieces of cut glass are safe to handle. The grinding wheel is coated with pieces of diamond and is lubricated with water from a reservoir under the grid. Always use protective glasses when you are working with the grinder, even if you have to put them on over your own glasses, as little glass fragments can fly off, or water containing ground glass can splash up into your face. Always check that there is water in the reservoir before you start grinding to protect the grinding wheel.

Light Box

The light box is not only used to select coloured glass, but also for a number of other functions including: tracing designs, painting, assembling the panel and looking at slides. The construction is quite basic: a box with a fluorescent light inside and a plate glass work surface, either sandblasted or with a piece of opaque plastic underneath to diffuse the light. The inside of the box is painted white with scrunched up silver foil placed between the light tubes for extra reflected light. An electrician might be able to help you construct one although a competent DIY enthusiast should find it easy to make.

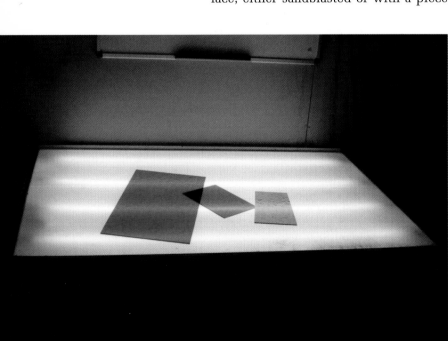

LEADING TOOLS

Soldering Iron

The soldering iron fuses the pieces of lead together that act as the 'glue' and holds the panel together. It is essential to buy a thermostatically-controlled soldering iron as this will give you the smoothest and fastest run and the best finish; it will also prevent you from inadvertently melting the lead, which is very difficult to repair.

Pliers and Oyster Knife

Pliers are used to stretch the lead and the oyster knife is extremely useful as it releases mangled lead wings and pushes glass into position, therefore saving your fingers from becoming lacerated and black.

Lead Cutters

Lead cutters come in several shapes, but I would recommend the chunky ones with the metal cap over the handle. They are by far the easiest to use and the metal handle can be used to hammer horseshoe nails into the board.

Lead Vice

The last thing you will need is a lead vice to stretch the lead, as shown in the next section.

MATERIALS

Glass

Glass is a liquid; but you need very high temperatures to see it flow freely. However, if you look at some medieval glass in church windows, you might see that some pieces of glass are thinner at the top than at the bottom as the glass has flowed very slowly downwards over hundreds of years.

It is also an extremely versatile material and can be used in space, communication technology (fibre optic cables), security (bullet-proof glass), science (test tubes), as well as everyday, household objects (television and computer screens, drinking vessels, light bulbs, cooking pots and optical glasses) – the list is endless. It can

be both fragile and extremely hard and is, overall, a most intriguing material.

Glass is made by heating a mixture of silica, sand, soda, ash and lime at very

Textured glass.

high temperatures. Metal oxides are then added when it is in this molten state to produce the colours. There are three methods of producing glass: the most traditional glass is mouth-blown into cylinders, snipped at both ends and cut length-wise so that it flattens under its own weight. The second method is hand-cast glass: the molten glass is poured onto a metal surface and rolled by hand to different thicknesses. The third method, also used in the production of commercial glass, is machine rolled: the glass is put on a conveyor belt and patterns are 'printed' into its surface, it is then rolled through different ovens to anneal it (stabilize it by slow cooling).

All these kinds of glass have a variety of characteristics. As a general rule, the hand-made glass is the most fragile and therefore the hardest to cut, especially when it is thick and has textures on both sides. It also has a lot of character with exquisite striations, swirls, streaks and the brightest colours. No two pieces of glass are the same and the textures and colours produced are the most distinctive characteristics.

The machine-made glass always has a smooth side and is easy to cut. However, it is also uniform and predictable; I therefore like to combine both kinds of glass to contrast and complement textures and colours.

When you begin choosing glass and looking at the bewildering choice, approach the supplier and ask for a catalogue to help you with your selection. Look at the glass on the shelf, feel its surface texture and study its qualities in the natural light. The best way to make your selection is to hand-pick it; hand-made glass comes in large sheets and you can show the shopkeeper which part of the sheet you would like him to cut.

Bear your design in mind and always have the glass cut with plenty in reserve in case of breakages during the cutting –

you will certainly use the leftover glass later. If you particularly like one kind of glass, cut a corner off the sheet and note down the code number for reference so you can then order it by phone later; this is much easier than trying to describe the colour and texture of the glass you need.

Although the choice of glass is often daunting, you can soon tell which types are the most appropriate to your design and fit your style. Most of all, follow your instincts and choose the glass that most appeals to you. The following is a rough guide to the kinds of glass you will come across:

Antique Glass

Antique glass is hand-made and can be characterized by its richness of colour, which often varies within a sheet, and its irregular texture, which often contains air bubbles.

Streaky Glass

Streaky glass is a variation of antique glass and has multiple swirls of colour running through it.

Flashed Glass

Flashed glass is a clear or light coloured antique glass with a thin, strong-coloured layer of glass fused onto one surface. It is used for acid-etching, engraving or sand blasting (*see* Project 3).

Reamy Glass

Reamy glass is an antique glass with watery swirls, an excellent glass to suggest movement and subtlety. It has soft or wild ridges, some also have air bubbles that are either clear or light in colour. A variety of this is Reamy Slab, a less irregularly textured glass, not as subtle but far cheaper.

Cathedral Glass

Cathedral glass is usually just a single, translucent colour with a surface texture and is machine-rolled or mouth-blown.

Seedy Glass

Seedy glass is a cathedral glass with a smooth surface and tiny air bubbles which trap sunlight brilliantly.

Opalescent Glass

Opalescent glass is opaque and diffuses and reduces light, which is why it is often used for making lampshades. However, avoid using it for windows as it tends to be rather brash in this context.

The above types of glass are the most expensive, as well as being the most intricate and exquisite in colour and texture, and the most irregular in thickness. The hand-made process means that some stresses creep into the glass and it can be rather temperamental when you try to cut it, so handle it with extra care.

The following types of glass are regular in texture as they are machine-made with one surface always smooth, or smoother than the textured surface. They have few stresses and are also a consistent thickness with no air bubbles. This makes them easier to cut but also means that they can appear flat and monotonous. However, they can make a perfect framework or background for the hand-blown glass in your design and are also considerably cheaper.

Semi-Antique Glass

Semi-antique glass is machine-made, usually translucent and has a regular antique-style pattern with a large variety of bright colours.

Glue Chip and Craquel

Glue chip and craquel are chemically treated types of glass with distressed surfaces.

Textured Art Glass

Textured art glasses like granite, muffle and flemish are machine-made glasses with distinctive, regular textures.

Textured Commercial Glass

Textured commercial glasses like stippolyte, matrix, arctic and taffeta are the types you would find in many buildings, both domestic and industrial, and are available from any glass supplier's catalogue. They are not traditionally used in stained glass panels, but can give your work a contemporary edge.

The last types of glass add relief to your work. These are jewel-like, pre-formed pieces and cannot be cut.

Bevels

Bevels are polished, pieces of glass used to refract rainbow colours (*see* Project 1).

Roundels

Roundels are circles of spun glass for achieving a period effect or any effect in a contemporary panel (*see* Project 2).

Globs and Nuggets

Globs and nuggets are irregular-shaped glass pebbles, available in all colours, from glass suppliers and flower shops.

Jewels

Jewels are often faceted and come in all shapes and sizes, they can be used in any panel, jewellery and lamps, but choose with care as they can look rather cheap when used in great quantities.

This list is by no means exhaustive and you need to keep looking around for new types of glass coming onto the market. New supplies are always being shipped in and the variety of hand-made glass is slowly increasing. Keep an eye on the catalogues and do not rely too heavily on the continuity of certain varieties of glass.

LEAD

For the beginner, providing you have a soldering iron, the easiest way to start assembling the glass into a panel is by using the copperfoil technique. Rolls of copperfoil tape are usually available in craft shops and you will also need some liquid flux, which comes in a plastic bottle and is an agent used to fuse the solder to the copperfoil.

The shiny sticks next to the flux in the photograph are the solder (40 per cent tin and 60 per cent lead) and these can also be used to solder the lead, of which there are examples in various widths next to the solder. The lead comes in 2m strings, or lead cames, and is only available from specialized glass suppliers. You can also buy different kinds of lead came: some are U-shaped in profile and are used as

USEFUL TIPS:

1 Cut a corner off each sheet that you want to restock, label it with the name and code number and glue each piece onto a clear sheet of glass for easy reference.
2 Check the thickness of the glass and how easy it will be to cut to avoid a difficult job later on.
3 If you want to paint onto the glass, make sure to choose a light colour.
4 Order generously to allow for any breakages, but monitor prices to ensure that you do not exceed your budget.
5 Do not be carried away by the seductive charm of a piece of glass for its own sake. Have your ideas or design project in mind so that you can make the glass fit the design, rather than the other way around.

the framework for decorative panels. Some of these are copper finished and can only be cut with a hacksaw. The most versatile cames, however, are the H-shaped ones and these are the ones that I use. The waxy material (tallow) in the middle of the photo is a piece of sheep's fat which is used as a flux for the lead.

Inevitably the lead gets a little twisted when it is being handled or transported but that can be rectified with the lead vice. This vice needs to be screwed down to a permanent structure and is used to stretch the lead to remove kinks and to make it more rigid.

The lead cames are H-shaped in cross-section and can have face widths from 3–22mm. The heart width is usually 1–2mm and the heart height is between 3–5mm. I usually use the 5mm heart height lead as it can accommodate all thicknesses of glass.

heart width

heart height

heart

face width

When ordering lead, or any materials for that matter, by order form, the message is simple: check, check and double check as it is easy to make an expensive mistake. The lead is sold in individual cames, or in mixed-length boxes of 50kg, which can be the cheapest way of buying them. Make sure that the lead cames do not get entangled and twisted by storing them carefully in a box. Be careful that you test an individual came before you buy a large quantity, as some are too soft to use successfully, and do look around for the best quality buy.

I have shown you the essential tools and materials with which you can make glorious panels and windows, providing that you start with a strong design; the following items are optional, but you may find them useful.

OPTIONAL TOOLS AND MATERIALS

The beauty of glass is, by now, surely indisputable. However, a long tradition of painting and etching on glass has demonstrated that even glass can be enhanced and enriched with appropriate painting and etching techniques. For me, it is this sophistication which gives glass a place amongst the greatest art forms.

PAINTING TOOLS

These tools are basically normal painting tools, although you will need to learn a new set of rules before you use them. Basic water-colour brushes are available from any art shop, whilst hard- and soft-bristled brushes can be found at glass suppliers. You will also need sticks for scratching away the paint, and cloths to wipe and texture the paint.

The large soft brushes, or badger brushes as they are called, are used to produce washes and blocks of colour and will produce the smoothest finish. I would suggest you have two badger brushes and use a separate one when applying a highly corrosive paint called silver stain.

The other essentials are a piece of plate glass with polished or ground edges to use as a palette to mix the paints, a palette knife, and plastic tubs to preserve the powdered paints and to stop them from getting damp.

Painting tools.

There are two kinds of glass kiln: gas-fired or electric. The gas-fired kiln is robust, reliable and economical to run. It also cools down quickly (in approximately 45 minutes) and the temperature does not go higher than 730°C, which means that glass cannot be fused or formed in this kiln. To do this you will need to invest in a laser kiln, which is computer-controlled and can be timed to switch on and off automatically and remain at a certain temperature for a pre-set time. This means that you can melt glass into all sorts of shapes, although this is a very different discipline and not

The Kiln

The kiln is used to fire paints into glass, or, if it fires at higher temperatures, to fuse or bend glass. This is the most expensive tool to buy, although you might find other local artists who would be willing to let you use their kiln. If you want to buy a kiln it is advisable to do some market research beforehand as there may be some bargains available.

There are two kinds of kiln you could use: the ordinary potter's kiln and the glass kiln; the potter's kiln is the more basic choice as it is harder to control the temperature. If possible choose a kiln with a kiln sitter, which is a device that holds a ceramic cone or stick; at a certain temperature the ceramic will melt and the attached spring will switch the kiln off automatically so that you do not have to worry about over- or under-firing your glass. However, this type of kiln is not as reliable as the glass kilns, as the glass can be unstable when it comes out and may shatter or crack.

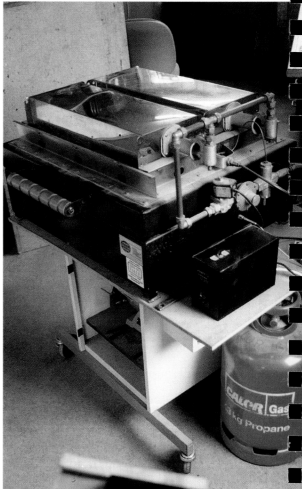

(Right) *A gas-fired kiln.*

for the faint-hearted or for people who want to achieve quick results.

Before you choose a kiln, try some out in a studio or a class and think carefully about how you want to use it. If you want to make jewel-like panels you will not need a large kiln, however, if you want to make large windows you will need a kiln with the largest shelf possible. You also need to consider accommodating the kiln in a space which can be aired safely; I have put my kiln on wheels so that it can be pulled away from the wall when in use.

PAINTING MATERIALS

There are basically three different types of paints, all of which are sold in powder form:

Tracing Colours

Tracing colours, also called oxides, are the oldest type of paints and date back to medieval times. The name 'tracing colour' refers to their original use; namely painting lines onto glass to fill in details such as faces and folds in material. They can also be used to shade, create textures and fill in blocks of colour in infinite tones. The colours are earthy and dull, varying from a pure black to opaque grey-green and white, and do not change colour in the kiln. The most commonly used colours are the black, brown and terracotta red (also called flesh red).

These paints are fired at high temperatures (650°C) and their advantage is that you can achieve great detail and fine graffiti effects; they can also all be mixed to achieve numerous shades of colour. You also have a lot of control as the paint does not change during firing, apart from taking on a dull gloss after firing.

When mixing, add a tiny drop of diluted gum arabic to make the paint easier to handle; this will also prevent you from accidentally rubbing it off the glass while you are working. The dried paint is only a layer of fine dust-like powder until it is fired into the glass.

A bridge comprising a smooth slat of wood with a block of wood screwed to

Tracing colours.

Using a bridge.

Enamels.

Enamels

Enamels are transparent or opaque bright colours which cannot be mixed. They are fired at low temperatures (590°C) and will change appearance during the firing process. Do be careful as these paints can change colour on coloured glass and always remember that the paints will *lighten* and become transparent or opaque during the firing process. It is therefore important to paint and fire all the different paints on a piece of clear glass. The corresponding name and code of the enamel should be scratched into each painted area before firing, as illustrated. Traditionally these paints are used on clear glass, which acts as an empty canvas, however, more interestingly, they can also be painted onto coloured glass. It is best used as a wash of colour. It clings better to the glass when dry than an oxide, so be sure not to use any gum arabic.

each end, will help to protect your paint-work as it prevents you from rubbing your hand against the paint while you work.

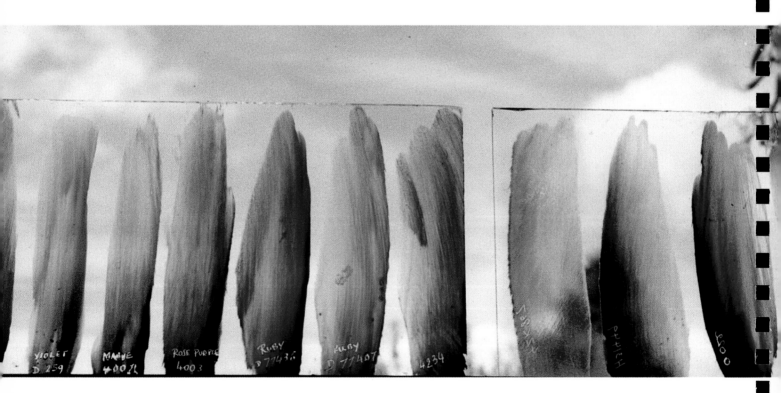

Silver Stains

Silver stains are both the most exquisite and the most difficult paints to use. The name refers to the silver nitrate, which reacts with the glass to make a golden colour when fired. The colours range from a light, soft yellow to a deep, rich amber, depending on the thickness of the paint. It is a low firing paint (like the enamels) and is corrosive because of the silver nitrate, so clean your palette knife and brushes very thoroughly after using it. Also be extremely careful not to lick your fingers as the paint is toxic.

The main difference from the previous paints is that you need to wash the layer of rust-coloured residue off the glass after firing to reveal the result. This is because, unlike the enamels and the oxides, this paint becomes part of the surface of the glass, rather than fired on top of the surface. The difficulty is that it

USEFUL TIPS:

1 Paints are toxic, so never eat, drink or smoke if you have been handling paints without washing your hands first.
2 When your favourite paint is out of stock, use a substitute.
3 The large manufacturers sell paint in large quantities but if you only need a little, find a few people to share the paint, and the costs, with.
4 Always store paint in air-tight containers to keep it dry, in jars with screw-top lids for example.
5 Keep a separate glass palette (a plate glass mixing surface approximately 250mm square) for each paint, so you can keep adding to the paint with the minimum of waste.
6 These paints are permanently fired, and not to be confused with cold paints, which are varnishes and cannot be fired.
7 These paints are not cheap, but they do last well, are great fun to use and create the most surprising results; they also give your work that professional edge.
8 Do not be impatient if you do not achieve immediate results. This is not an easy art so do experiment, and remember, you can start over again as often as you like, just wipe the paint off and start again.

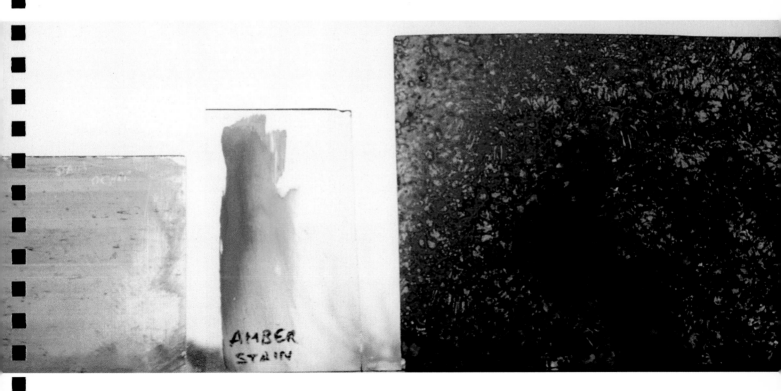

is hard to tell how the glass is going to react to the paint, although the advantage is that you can fire the paint face-down on the kiln shelf so you can paint on both sides of the glass before firing.

ETCHING TOOLS AND MATERIALS

Opaque Acid Etching

Frosting is the most straightforward technique and can be done in a small corner of the house. You will need a tub of velvet etching cream (*see* Projects 3 and 7), some water, rags and nylon painting brushes. You should also wear protective gloves as the acid can burn your skin.

The paste is brushed onto the glass and reacts immediately with the surface to form a sandblasted, opaque effect. It

A frosted motif on a greenhouse.

has a very smooth, silky touch and traps the light in a luminous way, especially against a dark background. The effect is flat when the paste is applied as a solid coverage, or smoky if brushed on loosely, so experiment with these effects on some scrap glass before you start. This simple motif (*see* below) has been frosted onto the window of a greenhouse.

If you want to achieve a more varied, opaque, etching effect you will need to use a sandblasting tool, which is a large industrial cabinet with a motor (or compressor) and a dust collector. Some colleges and glass suppliers will rent these machines out by the hour, however, this is a whole new technique which is not covered in this book.

Clear Acid Etching

You will need a bottle of hydrofluoric acid, a photographer's development tray and grips, some large bird's feathers, a plastic container with funnel to store the diluted acid and a large bucket of water. Do make sure that the bottle of acid is stored carefully in a dark, cool space.

This process can be done at home, providing you have a large enough space outside, as the fumes coming off the acid are quite toxic. Alternatively, if you are going to practise this technique indoors then you will need a powerful ventilation system, which requires a lot of space and could mean considerable extra cost.

Start by collecting the materials to prepare your glass for etching. If you want to achieve a clear-edged motive, use self-adhesive clear plastic film, if you want a loose, organic, flowing effect, use a stop out varnish (*see* Project 3) and the glass will etch out clear.

Always wear protective glasses and an old shirt or long plastic apron when handling acids. The first step is to dilute the acid (add about 40 per cent water);

Materials needed for clear acid etching.

always add the acid to the water when you are not diluting, *never* the other way around as the acid will splash and spit; remember you can always dilute it further if the etching process is happening too fast for you.

Be sensible, concentrate and make sure that you are properly protected before you start. Avoid splashing at all costs and have a bucket of water close at hand to plunge your hands into in case some acid accidentally drips onto them; the acid will start reacting to your skin in approximately thirty seconds so you have a little time. Obviously you should avoid splashing acid on your glasses, let alone into your eyes, however, if this does happen, rinse your eyes with running water and seek medical help. The main advice I can give is that if you are relaxed and sensible while handling acid there is little danger.

Engraving

Engraving is a wonderful technique for emphasizing small details and is ideal for adding little touches and tidying up etched glass; however it is not suitable for making great statements on a large panel. A small, electric, hobby-style glass engraver is suitable for most jobs, although in Project 4 you can see an application using a more sophisticated version. That particular tool is great for intricate drawing, which is an art in itself.

CREATING AN ARTIST'S STUDIO

If you do not have a purpose-built space, you will need to convert a corner of your house. The dining room table is not a happy solution and neither is the loft if there is no proper insulation, ventilation or water supply. A spare bedroom, often a popular candidate, is fine as long as you do not have guests, however a shed, or a room with easy access into the garden or hobby room is a better choice. If possible there should also be running water, plenty of plug sockets, good natural light and a cleanable floor (linoleum is ideal). Make sure you have permanent storage space to lock away tools and materials safely as children and pets can be very nosy.

Do make sure that you allow enough space for stretching lead, a permanent

fixture to screw your vice onto and a large enough wall space to store the larger sheets of glass.

Layout

Position a waist-high work surface near to a window, or, alternatively, underneath a fluorescent tube. You will need plenty of space for the lead as it should not be folded; if you can stack it on a shelf system then it will be easily accessible and take up a minimum amount of space. Alternatively, it can be stored in a new guttering pipe, available from any DIY store, attached along the wall, open side uppermost. Keep all the glass more or less on one shelf system and have a pile of containers to hand for the bits of coloured glass you would like to keep. Larger sheets of glass should be stored vertically. Use drawers for your designs and drawing tools, find a place to keep rags and newspapers and create shelf space for your tools; the first aid kit should also be within easy reach. If you have a kiln, place it near a window and onto a hard, durable surface (not onto thick pile carpet).

My studio has two north-facing windows (ideal for natural light), an east-facing glass wall with adjustable horizontal sub-divisions to hold the glass easels and panels, and a west-facing window. The work benches are positioned under the north windows, and the lightbox, lead and glass storage are all by the blind wall for easy access; I also like to keep some wall space for hanging up my designs. There are also several rubbish bins dotted around and I keep a broom handy to sweep up the heavy-duty linoleum floor. I do not claim that this is the ideal layout for a professional studio, but it suits me and I do change things around occasionally to accommodate my changing needs; it is a working space.

(Opposite) The author's studio: east facing (above) and west facing (below).

SAFETY TIPS:

Whatever you do, just be sensible and you are ninety-nine per cent safe. Be relaxed when handling all tools, but also on your guard. You may find the following tips helpful:

1. To handle glass safely, treat it with respect at all times. When picking it up grab it firmly, but carefully. Support larger sheets of glass from underneath.
2. Off-cuts of glass in a container often have sharp corners so use gloves, or pick through them carefully.
3. When cutting glass, cut on top of a sheet of paper to catch the glass chips and shake them into a bin regularly.
4. Keep a supply of plasters handy; you will cut yourself and it is always better to be prepared. Always wash your hands before putting on the plaster.
5. When you are painting, leading or handling glass, do not eat, smoke or put your fingers into your mouth.
6. When soldering lead, avoid breathing the fumes as they are toxic and ensure that the work-space is well ventilated by opening windows or doors. A build-up of fumes can cause dizziness which can be dangerous if you are operating any kind of machinery and is harmful to anyone who suffers respiratory problems or to pregnant women.
7. Concentrate while soldering as absentmindedness can cause nasty burns.
8. Keep all areas as clean as possible; glass fragments get everywhere.
9. Do not wear contact lenses while working, your ordinary glasses will give you better protection.
10. If you have long hair tie it back out of your face, avoid wearing dangly jewellery and never wear high heels while you work.

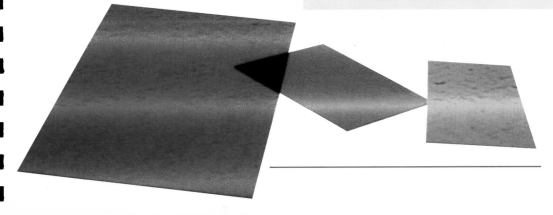

4 Projects

The following projects are tailor-made to show a range of techniques. They start with a fairly simple panel, move through to three-dimensional objects and end with an architectural window. I will introduce you to new techniques with every project, or mix several techniques to create an effect. By introducing painting, acid-etching, frosting, copperfoil technique, fusing and engraving I hope to give you the inspiration to create exciting works. You can try all the projects and adapt them to suit your own facilities. This is a flexible medium so you can vary the theme, change your mind in the cutting process and substitute one kind of glass for another; once you start leading or copperfoiling however, the final decision has been made.

PROJECT 1

THE GEOMETRIC PANEL

EQUIPMENT:

- Drawing tools, pencils, colour pencils, water-soluble felt-tip pens

- A selection of bevels, clear textured glass, coloured glass

- Lead of different face widths (from 2–10mm wide), solder, tallow

- All purpose putty, black grate polish

- Metal wire, keyring holders, brass chain, horseshoe nails

Start by drawing a design onto paper indicating colours and shapes, as shown in the illustration. Avoid drawing lines from one border to the next as this makes for a weak structure; a strong structure is grid-like. You will need to ensure that your bevels fit precisely into your design as they are pre-cut. Draw the outline or lead line in felt-tip pen; this is your cartoon and you need to be precise otherwise you will not end up with a square panel.

Copy your cartoon onto the glass easel (this is a piece of plate glass 4mm thick with ground or smooth edges) with a water-soluble pen (this makes it easier to wash off afterwards). I recommend that

Initial design drawings.

you turn over your cartoon and copy the mirror image onto the easel as you will avoid smudging the lines while you work. Use a light box as the back of your cartoon will then show through the paper.

Select the glass roughly for the different areas; you can still change it as you go along. Trace each shape of glass with a thin felt-tip pen within the lines on your glass easel, making sure that you leave a few millimetres gap between each piece of glass to allow for the heart of the lead; always think a few steps ahead.

Cut each piece of glass as economically as possible; you will waste less glass by tracing as far into the corner of the sheet as you can. Start by cutting off the rest of the sheet; always cut on the smoothest side of your glass and remember to dip the head of your cutter in oil for a smooth finish. Cut from one edge of your sheet to the next to be sure of a clean break.

To break a straight score (score is the line you have cut into the glass), use the glass breaker, but for smaller pieces like these the grozing pliers are easier to use. Always work on a sheet of white paper so that you catch all the little glass chips and occasionally shake them into the bin so that you avoid cutting yourself.

Press your piece of cut glass firmly into position with little pieces of re-usable adhesive or mastic; use at least three pieces to prevent it from slipping. If you need to grind a sharp edge, dry the glass thoroughly so that your mastic will stick. Hold your easel vertically up to the light in between to check that you have achieved the desired effect. When using clear textured glass, switch off the light box so that you can see the result.

Once you have cut and positioned all your pieces of glass, check that you have enough spaces in between the pieces to allow for the heart of the lead; you can still change some of the glass at this stage. When holding your easel up to a window you will notice that a background setting makes the glass textures come alive, whereas a plain sky flattens the textures.

To start the leading, place your cartoon onto the assembly board, allowing enough space on the edge for the border lead, and cut about 5mm away from two sides of your cartoon; fix it down with masking tape. The assembly board consists of a piece of plywood with wooden battens screwed to two sides of the board.

Before the lead can be used, it needs to be stretched using the lead vice which uncoils and toughens it. Clamp one end of the came into the vice and grab the other end with the pliers. You will need

Stretching the lead.

to use some muscle but do not lean backwards; balance your body by spreading your legs so that you do not fly backwards if the lead came snaps or slips.

Decide how wide you would like the border to be – I used an 8mm wide lead – and cut two pieces of lead to size for the border, holding them into position against the battens with horse nails. Cut them slightly longer than your cartoon suggests and start by putting the glass from the bottom left-hand corner in first. If you are left-handed, you should start off in the bottom right-hand corner. Push the glass firmly into the border lead grooves and then mark the next piece of lead. Mitre the lead so that there is no gap with the adjoining border lead and do make sure that you have selected the right widths so that you are consistent throughout the piece. Your lead needs to fit snugly into the glass and be pinned into position with horseshoe nails at all times. You may have to wiggle the lead in, using your oyster knife, but mind your fingers, as the lead can cut into them.

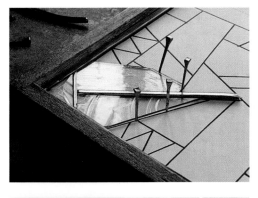

Creating the design on the assembly board.

(Below) *Exposing the silvery shine of the lead with a wire brush.*

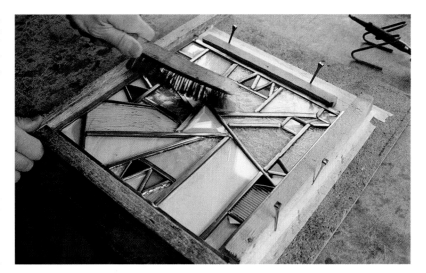

As you can see from this sequence (*see above*), I use a variety of lead widths. I call it 'drawing with the lead'. Keep an eye on the overall effect and always think a few steps ahead. Where the glass meets a new piece of lead, cut your previous lead a little shorter to allow for overlapping and decide which width you will use next to avoid gaps. Each design is different so use your common sense to see what your next step should be.

When all the pieces have been glazed in, the two remaining borders are gently tapped into position with loose battens; use your ruler to make sure the panel is square and adjust by tapping. Plug in your soldering iron to heat up and brush all the lead joints with a wire brush to take away the oxidized grey surface and expose the silvery shine of the lead.

Rub each joint with a touch of tallow; if you still have some gaps where the joints should be, push in some little wedges of lead to bridge the gap. It will become invisible with a layer of solder on top, providing you cut your wedges to the right size; it is fiddly, but essential for a good finish.

Rubbing each joint with a touch of tallow.

the leftovers to solder together for re-use. When you have soldered every joint, carefully turn your piece around and do the same on the reverse side. You will find that, at this stage, the panel is wobbly, as the thinner pieces of glass are rattling in their lead case.

For the cementing process, I use all-purpose putty which is mixed with a little black grate polish; you can buy tubs of glazing cement at suppliers, but I find that they dry out too quickly. When storing putty, keep it tightly sealed to stop it from drying out. You can rub the cement into the grooves with your hands or with a brush if the panel is bolder; keep the putty wet so that it flows in. The cementing will make your panel firm and waterproof. Repeat this process on the reverse side.

When your soldering iron has heated up, melt your stick of solder in the middle otherwise it will be too long to handle comfortably; open a window if possible to get rid of the fumes. Use as little solder as possible, melting it on top of the joint without touching the lead for a few seconds until it has smoothed out. When your stick of solder gets hot, it will be too short to use so start a new stick and keep

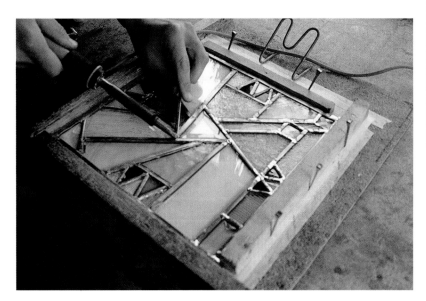

Brush a small amount of chalk onto the panel in circular movements; too much chalk will result in clouds of dust. This will push the cement further into the grooves and polish the grease off the glass. Work on top of newspaper for these messy stages so you do not

The right amount will turn the lead a satin black and the glass will shine.

As you can see (below), the blacking has cleaned the glass beautifully. The finishing touch is to clean away the last excesses of putty, pushed out during the polishing process, using a sharpened stick or anything to hand. This is called picking. The cement will dry in a day and harden in the following weeks.

The last process is to solder metal hooks into the grooves of the border by flowing the solder onto the wires and filling the grooves. Extend the wire by at least a third into the border lead and attach any chain to the wire loops with keyring hangers. This panel can now be hung in any window space.

The finished piece. Excess putty is being cleaned away.

cover your whole working space in a sticky mess.

Wire brush the lead and simultaneously rub the excess cement off the glass. Squeeze a little blacking onto a soft brush or directly onto your panel and rub it into the lead; this will also clean your glass further but if you use too much blacking your panel will become greasy and dull.

PROJECT 2

THE PAINTED, CURVILINEAR PANEL

EQUIPMENT:

- Black tracing paint, silver stain, palette knife, glass palette, brushes, badger brushes, a kiln

- A roundel, white reamy glass, blue art glass, clear industrial glass and the tools used in Project 1

(N.B. the same tools are used in all the projects)

When you have cut your glass and tacked it to your glass easel, you are ready to paint. Prepare your paint by mixing it with a few drops of water, making sure your palette is clean before you start. You can mix a drop of diluted gum arabic into it if you want to store or transport your painted glass before firing. Use the high-firing paints first, and, as always, as this paint is particularly toxic, make sure wash your hands if you touch it.

Mix the paint well to the consistency of single cream; by grinding the paint while you mix, you will get rid of the graininess of the powder.

Paint the pieces in sections so that the process is easier to control and keep your colour design to hand so that you can keep checking your work. Use round water colour brushes to paint the washes onto the glass and keep the paint quite wet by dipping your brush into your

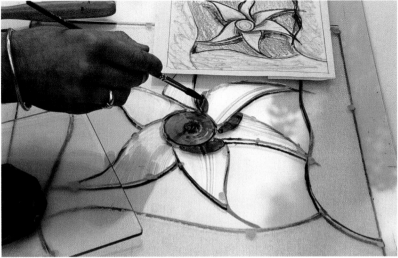

water pot. You can paint quite roughly at this point, covering more than the area you want to paint, as you will be scraping some away later. While you are painting remember that you need to work on wet paint, so work swiftly to avoid the paint drying out while you are brushing it and work on small areas at a time. If the paint separates into drops, your glass will be too greasy; wash the glass with soap and rinse well or slop some watery paint onto the glass and wipe dry.

Use the badger brush on the *wet* paint to achieve the desired thickness; if you use the light box you will be able to see the thickness of the paint. For an even wash of colour, brush in all directions, for a graded effect, brush predominantly in one direction. Use only the tip of the brush, otherwise the brush will get too soggy and will create a rough, stripy finish; it will take some practice to create a smooth finish so do not give up too soon. When you have finished, let the badger brush dry and flick off the powder.

When the paint has dried, start the graffiti by scraping the paint away; you can use hard bristled brushes for a sharp linear effect or soft brushes for a softer, feathery effect. When you are happy with your painting, put this section in the kiln and start the next section, so that you do not disturb the finished painted areas.

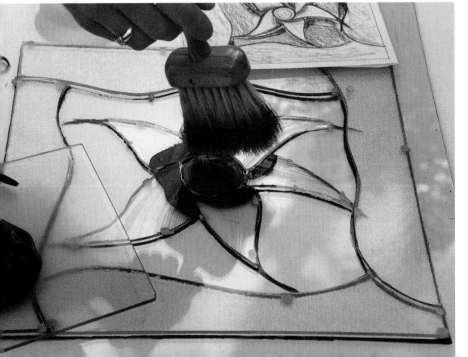

After firing the oxides at 650°C the next section can be painted. I usually paint on top of the fired black paint, as well as the frame, using the silver stain. Use a clean brush and a different badger brush and palette knife as this will prevent the silver stain from contaminating your tools. The same painting techniques apply but this paint is less forgiving; when used very watery, it separates and when used thick, it tends to take on the consistency of treacle. It can be hard to tell how thick the layer of paint is and it can also be unpredictable in the firing.

Put the glass into the kiln when dry, and cook for three minutes at 590°C.

However, there is also a positive side to using this paint; you can create exciting effects by splattering drops of paint onto the half-dried layer of paint which will create crevices and artery-type configurations. The effects can be mesmerizing so use the paint as haphazardly as you can.

Wash the paint after firing and it will reveal the golden finish under the rusty-coloured residue.

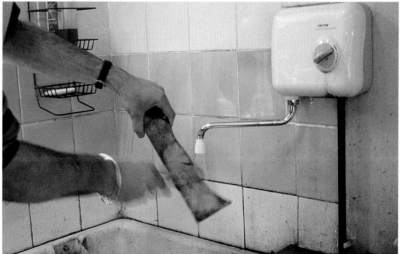

PROJECT 3

FREE-FORM ACID ETCHED PANEL

EQUIPMENT:

◆ Diluted hydrofluoric acid, feathers, photographer's tray, stop out varnish, velvet acid paste, turpentine, nylon brushes, contact paper

◆ Flashed, sandblasted and clear glass, paints

Draw your cartoon and prepare the sandblasted glass for acid etching; sandblasted glass is readily available at all glass merchants. Cut out the clear contact paper (self-adhesive plastic film) slightly bigger than your piece of glass.

Stretch the clear contact paper over the glass, slowly peeling off the backing paper and firmly rubbing the contact film onto the glass, making sure that no air bubbles are trapped between the glass and the plastic. Run your scalpel across the edge, trimming off the excess. Turn around and repeat on the reverse

side and then rub the film tightly onto the edges using a cloth.

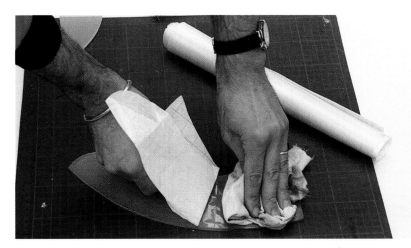

Cut out the motives on the blasted (opaque) side and remove the slips to reveal the area to be acid-etched. Press the surrounding plastic and edges down firmly so that no acid can flow underneath. Now prepare all the other glass to be acid-etched.

Cut the flashed glass, scoring it on the back, not on the flashed side. You can tell which is the flashed side by holding the profile of the glass to the light or by

grinding or chipping a corner of the sheet. Stretch the contact film over the back side and then paint the varnish onto the flashed side of the glass, diluting it in parts with turpentine to make blurred edges.

Carefully pour the acid into the tray without splashing and, as always when you are working with acid, wear protective clothing and glasses and work either outside or in a professionally ventilated room as the fumes are quite harmful. When working outside, do make sure that there is enough daylight for you to see what you are doing.

Sink the glass into the acid bath with your gripping tools and gently rock the tray to speed up the process. Use the feather to wipe the glass residue off the piece of glass. This process will take between fifteen and fifty minutes approximately, depending on the thickness of the glass, the strength of the acid (acid will gradually lose its strength through use and exposure to light) and the temperature (the warmer the weather, the faster it will react). You can take the glass out of the acid bath occasionally, rinse it with water and check to see how far it has been etched by holding it to the sky. Take the glass out of the tray halfway through the process.

To speed up the drying process, use a hair dryer; in warmer weather the varnish will harden faster.

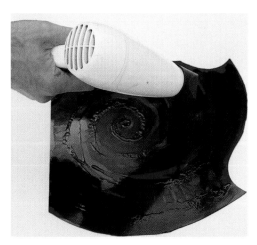

Rinse the glass and dry it thoroughly. Stretch contact paper over it and cut out the star motive. Put the glass back into

and then paint the sandblasted glass on the smooth side and fire all the pieces.

the acid until the result is to your satisfaction. Now etch the sandblasted glass.

Paint the silver stain onto the back, first wiping off the excess paint with a damp tissue, then sharpening the edges with a wooden point (I use the back of an old hairless brush).

Brush on some velvet etching cream with a nylon brush to bring out highlights and link the sandblasted glass with the flashed centrepiece. Wash off after a few minutes being careful to avoid splashing your skin with the acid.

Lead this irregularly-shaped piece by using plenty of nails to support and hold the lead in the glass; this is trickier to do than on a square piece but is a good challenge. Hang it using nylon fishing line for a light touch.

After the silver stain has dried, turn the piece around and paint the blue enamel on top of the etched flash to strengthen your motive. Use the badger brush on the paint to soften the edges

PROJECT 4

ENGRAVED MIRROR

EQUIPMENT:

- ◆ Glass engraver, circular glass cutter, mirror, masking fliud

- ◆ Coloured lens, mirror glass (3mm), coloured glass

Cut your mirror glass with a circular glass cutter; press the end of the cutter firmly on the mirror side of the glass with your thumb and tighten the screw on the cutting wheel to the desired length (24cm diameter). Swing the wheel end round loosely to track the cutting line and make sure there are no obstacles to prevent a smooth cutting movement. Press firmly on the wheel and cut the glass all in one go.

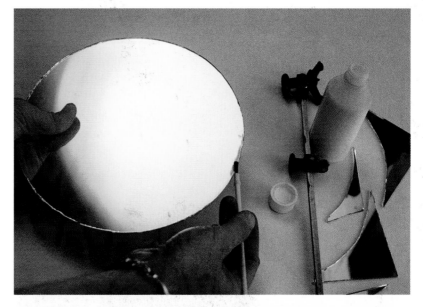

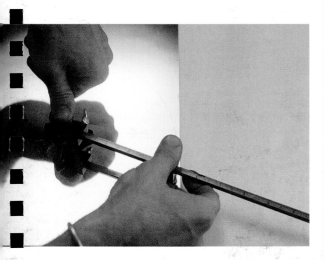

Brush the edges with mirror masking fluid to prevent corrosion and leave to dry by balancing on supporting blocks to prevent the edges sticking to the table.

Cut the squares of glass and mirror using one template, making sure that the pieces of glass meet at the top.

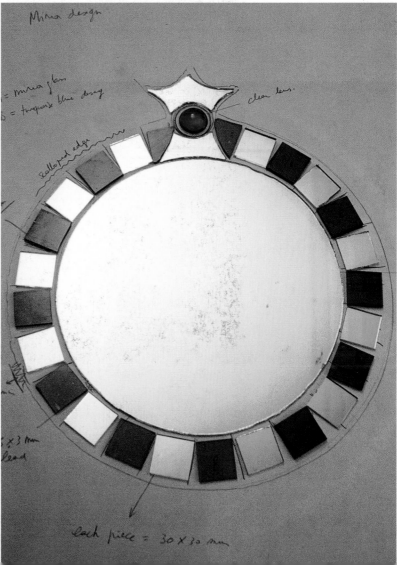

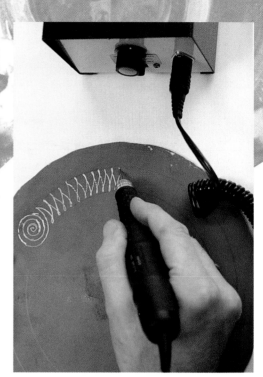

Engrave the back of the mirror, making sure that the light is visible through the graphic line. I start by drawing a guide line onto the back of the mirror, this is not easy to do this with a compass as the pin slips on the surface, so I use self-adhesive pads to hold it in position.

Cut equal pieces of lead to fit between the little 'tiles' of glass and mirror. Hold the mirror in position with nails, shifting them each time your framework moves to the next nail.

Flute the edge of the mirror by pressing the side of the oyster knife into the lead.

Solder wire hooks onto the back, inside the mirror frame, making sure that the solder covers the wire well. The hooks should be at the same height on both sides.

Attach a small chain, making sure that it does not show when it is hanging on the wall; you could also use picture wire.

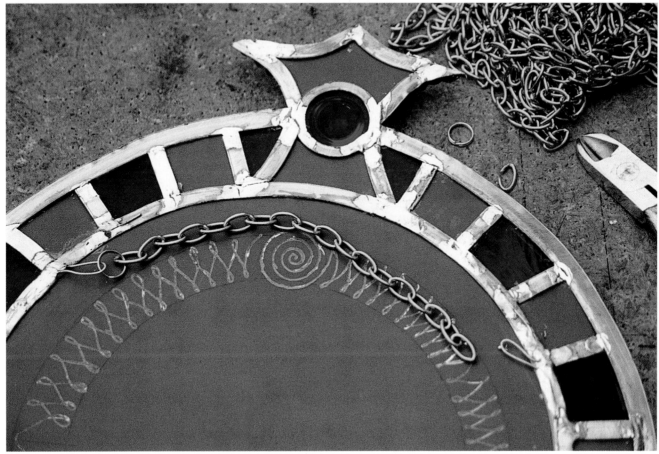

PROJECT 5

FUSED CANDLESTICK

EQUIPMENT:

◆ Glass fusing medium, copperfoil, solder, fluid solder flux, kiln

◆ Glass of your choice, nuggets, lead came (8mm width)

Cut the glass to your chosen shape, making sure that the top of each piece is not wider than 30mm, and the bottom is wider than the top (75mm in this case). The height is 240 millimetres in this example. Cut a free shape out of the

same sheet of glass to ensure successful firing; glass will only anneal or stabilize during fusing if the fusing pieces are compatible. If you use different kinds of glass, there will almost certainly be a stress in one of the pieces and the glass will shatter sooner or later. If you want to use compatible glass in a range of colours, you can buy pieces which have been tested as compatible.

Brush the sides of the glass you want to fuse together using the overglaze; this fluid is a fine, low melting, powdered glass, mixed with alcohol and water to ensure a smooth fuse. If you use it pure, it will add some textural quality, if you water it down it will seamlessly fuse together. Fire in a high firing kiln at between 780 and 840°C. At temperatures over 800°C, the pieces of glass will start to melt into one another and have round edges.

Measurements for each side of candlestick.

30mm

30mm

copper foil band

240mm

75mm

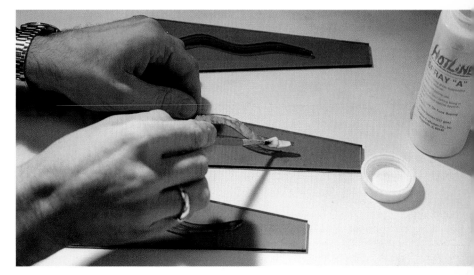

If you use a top-loading kiln you will find that the pieces on the top shelf are fused deeper into the glass. Try and fuse all pieces on the same shelf or as close as possible, to ensure all sides of the candlestick have the same fused finish.

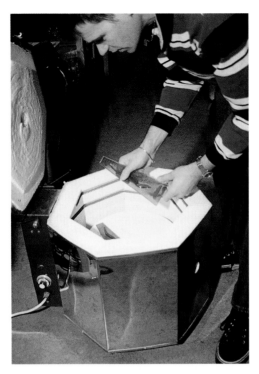

Placing the glass in a top-loading kiln.

will have the fused glass relief; this strip will hold the candle wax holder.

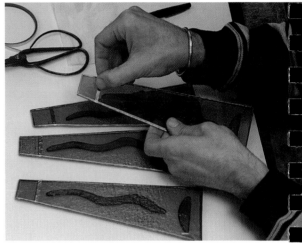

Secure two sides of the candlestick with masking tape and brush liquid flux onto the join, then tack the two sides together with the solder in several places across the join. Measure the inside of the candlestick at the height of the strip of copperfoil for the candle wax catcher. Cut a square of window glass (2–3mm thick) slightly smaller than your measurement suggests and wrap with copperfoil. Solder the square into position.

Lathekin: used to widen the channels in the lead cane (also for burnishing copperfoil).

Wrap the copperfoil around the edge of each piece, rubbing it firmly with lathekin. The glass should be grease-free to make sure that the self adhesive tape sticks to it.

Stick a strip of copperfoil on the inside of each piece (35mm from the top). The inside is the side which is flat, the outside

Attach the two remaining sides and fill the joins with solder by flowing it from the top, using enough flux to make it run smoothly. All the copperfoil should be covered in solder and any solder that drips onto the glass can then be easily peeled off.

You can smooth the solder down or make a decorative corner by melting the solder every 3–5mm in a horizontal position. You can also drop little 'pearls' of solder onto the soldered corners at regular intervals, or create a drip effect by melting the solder in an upward position.

After covering the top in solder, make the candle holder by coiling a piece of lead came around a solid round object, checking the size using a piece of candle. Solder the ends together and solder the lead ring onto the top of the candlestick.

Use a good epoxy glass glue to stick on the nuggets but do not use the infra-red bonding glue for dark glass.

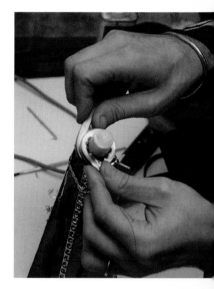

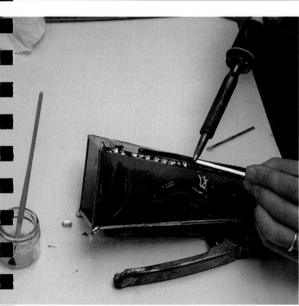

PROJECT 6

PYRAMID LAMP

EQUIPMENT:

◆ Lead came (3mm in width and 4mm in depth), solder and wire, a 13mm threaded entry, brass lamp holder, a 3-core flexible cable and a 5-Amp through-switch (connect by following the instructions on the packaging)

Cut and prepare the glass by cutting four identical pieces to form the sides of the lamp. The red flashed glass has been acid-etched using the self-adhesive clear film (*see* Project 3). The clear glass is English muffle which I have painted with silver stain. These pieces were frosted on the back using frosting cream: mask the glass with the clear film and brush it liberally with the cream; the same effect can also be achieved by sandblasting the glass. The opaque glass on the top of the pyramid is sandblasted glass; I used yellow glass for the fourth piece and a ruby nugget.

To lead each side of the lamp, use batons on the assembly board making sure that they are hammered down securely. As you cannot reach the outer corners easily with the soldering iron, solder the joins you can reach and then turn the piece round and solder the other side securely (you do not need the batons now); finally turn, and solder the corners on the front.

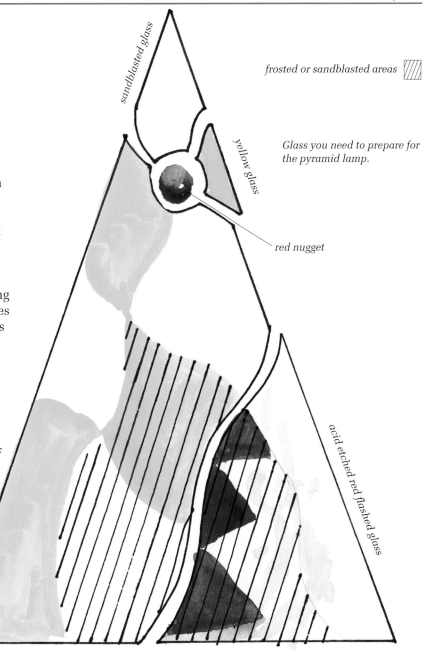

sandblasted glass

yellow glass

frosted or sandblasted areas ////

Glass you need to prepare for the pyramid lamp.

red nugget

muffle glass with silver stain

acid etched red flashed glass

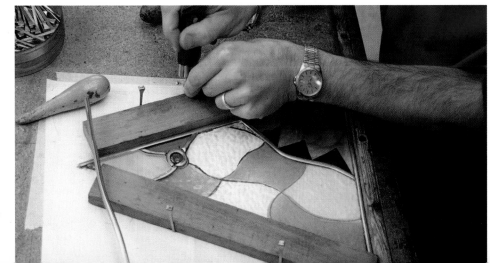

When you have leaded all four sides, wash the inside of each leaded piece, taking care to remove all grease from the frosted or sandblasted surface. Wire-brush the edging lead thoroughly on all sides to prepare it for the solder.

Tape the sides into position with masking tape and then hold the leaded pieces together by nailing batons onto the two remaining sides on the assembly board. Use plenty of tallow and flow the solder into the corners; if the solder does not flow well, brush again with the wire brush.

Use wire to secure the lamp holder by twisting it around the threaded neck of the lamp holder and securing with the screw ring. Secure each end to two adjacent corners of the lamp; the wire will not be tight at this stage but, when it is stretched tight, the lamp holder should be in the middle of the foot of the pyramid.

Melt a hole near the bottom of one corner of the pyramid with the soldering iron, pull the cable through the hole and carefully melt the lead again around the hole.

Repeat the procedure of wiring the lamp holder to the corners on the opposite side, but this time you can stretch it into place. Do not worry if it is slightly bouncy, as the lamp holder needs to be flexible in order to stand the lamp on a surface.

The finished lamp.

PROJECT 7

ARCHITECTURAL WINDOW

EQUIPMENT:

◆ Ruler, compass, felt-tip pens

◆ Textured glass, clear glass

The last project combines most of the techniques described previously, however there is one main difference: this piece will be fixed into the fabric of a building; it will influence the space and therefore needs to be carefully thought out.

The function of this particular window was to provide privacy, so I used densely-textured glass. The other brief was that it should let in plenty of light as it was going to be situated in the middle of a kitchen/dining area. I used plenty of

clear glass and also threw in some fresh, bright colours and added lenses for a playful touch. The design is contemporary and dynamic, to reflect the character of the commissioner.

Once the design has been approved, convert it to scale, using a ruler, compass and calculator. First draw the real outline of the windows with a felt-tip pen, then draw a line inside that border, with a 9mm space in between; this space will allow for the lead frame of the window. It is essential that the measurement of the window is precise as the design is presented to scale, so, when you are measuring, make sure you include the width of the beading, or, if there is no beading, the width of the putty border.

Once the main lines are drawn hang the cartoon on the wall to fill in the large curvilinear lines. Hanging it in a vertical position will enable you to see the overall effect and make adjustments to the original design. As the design is scaled up, the feeling shifts, so I do not

bother to photocopy it. Use string to draw the larger curves and allow yourself plenty of room.

The oxide paint is brushed on freely, smoothed out with a badger brush and left to dry; on warmer days or in a heated room work swiftly as the paint will dry quickly. The graphic marks are made with a sharpened wooden stick or any pointed object. Use a soft bristled stippler to achieve a soft fading of the painted, textured border.

The reverse of the cartoon is now transferred onto the reverse of the light easel in water-based pigment ink, using the light box.

Painted enamels and silver stain before firing (above) *and after firing* (below).

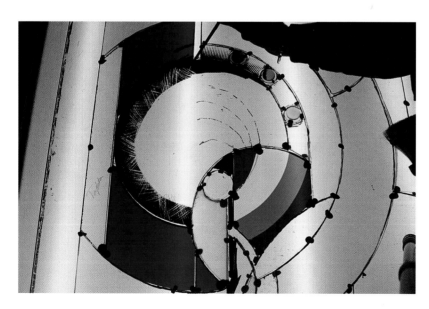

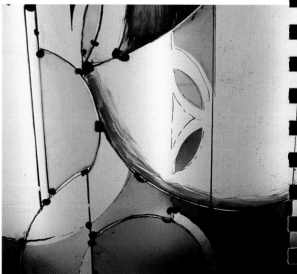

These effects will give the window extra depth and a soft feathery effect to contrast with the leaded outlines.

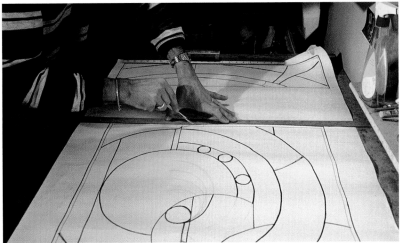

Enamels and silver stains change colour by firing in the kiln, they also lighten giving a wonderful array of effects (*see* photographs on previous page).

When using etching cream, always protect your skin by wearing gloves; mask around the area you want to frost using self adhesive clear plastic. This effect was created by using the cream in a patchy pattern on the outside of the circle.

The engraver is used to cross-hatch on the reverse side of the frosted area.

Two sides of the cartoon are cut on the outer line and fitted against the slats on the assembly board and taped down; check the size again.

Prepare the lead by stretching it and line up all the different widths you intend to use. If you are right-handed, it

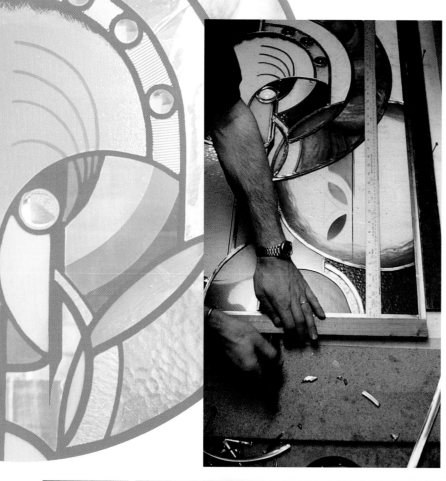

is easiest to start in the bottom left-hand corner and the last piece of glass to lead will be in the top right-hand corner.

Use battens to pin down the borders and tap them gently to settle the lead, then, with the help of a ruler, manoeuvre the panel into its precise size and shape.

When you are leading make sure that the room is properly ventilated. Use the smallest amount of solder you can get away with to avoid lumpiness; the blacking of the lead used afterwards will cover up any minor mistakes.

When turning the panel to solder the back, swivel it onto the floor in a vertical position and turn it around holding the top firmly.

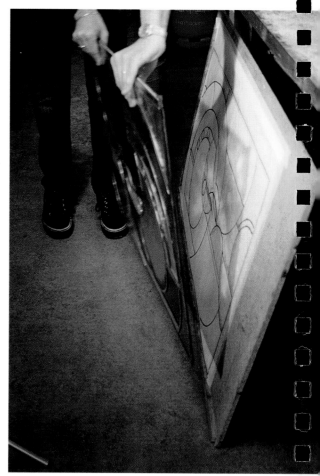

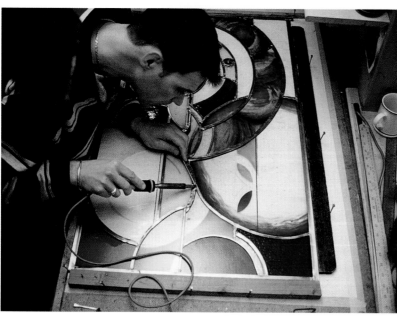

TROUBLESHOOTING TIPS

Q. Why does my glass keep breaking in the wrong direction?

A. Always cut on the smoothest side of the glass. If your glass cutter has been used many times, change it if it is a disposable one or change the wheel if possible.

  Did you cut at a 90° angle and did the scoring make an unbroken, high, soft crackling sound? If so, then there is no need to worry.

  Did you cut from one edge of the glass to another? You cannot cut a shape straight out of the middle of a piece of glass, but should gradually cut away the glass around the shape you need to cut.

Q. I keep cutting the lead came too short.

A. Cut the lead a little longer than you think it should be. Measure your piece of lead by positioning it above the cutting line with your glass pieces in place and mark with the lead cutter. Always remember to keep enough space to accommodate the piece of lead that will cross the lead you are cutting. Think a few steps ahead.

Q. My pieces of glass keep shifting around as I am trying to lead up.

A. Use plenty of nails and nail down each piece of glass when you have leaded it into position.

Q. My glass does not fit into the lead channels.

A Use lead with a heart height greater than the thickness of the thickest glass you are using; if you use 4mm glass, the heart height of the lead should be 5mm.

Q. The wings of my lead keep getting caught.

A. Widen the channels by running the lathekin inside them.

Q. My panel is not square.

A. Either you have not taken enough care when cutting the glass – you need to be as precise as possible – or, when you have leaded all the pieces before soldering, use battens to tap the whole piece gently into a square; the glass will then 'settle' into position.

Q. My solder will not run smoothly and is lumpy.

A. Use as little solder as possible to avoid lumps and wire brush the joins thoroughly; use extra flux if the solder does not run properly. Remember to ventilate the room properly to avoid a build-up of hazardous fumes.

Q. My copperfoil will not stick onto the glass.

A. Remove all grease from the glass with soap and dry thoroughly. The sides of your glass should be smooth enough for the copperfoil to stick (not jagged). Press down well with lathekin on all sides, including the overlaps.

(continued overleaf)

TROUBLESHOOTING TIPS (continued)

Q. My paints do not flow onto the glass and I cannot paint a continuous line.

A Remove all grease from the glass using some watered-down paint and wipe off with a clean cloth. When you paint onto the glass, the water in the paint evaporates quickly, due to the heat of the light box and the temperature in the room. If you want to paint on a wet surface work swiftly for a watery effect.

Q. My painted work keeps chipping off and unsightly lumps appear when it is fired.

A. You are using the paint too thickly. Do not paint layer upon layer without firing the first layer of paint in between. Apply layers of colour to slowly build up a rich texture.

Q. When I use the etching cream, the effect is always patchy.

A. Use more cream to cover the glass thoroughly and leave the acid on the glass longer.

Q. The contact sheet floats off in the acid bath before it can be etched.

A. Before you stick on the plastic, remove all grease from the glass. When you are sticking the plastic down, start on one side of the glass and peel off a corner of the backing paper and gradually smooth the self-adhesive sheet onto the glass by firmly rubbing it on. If you gradually peel of the backing paper you will avoid air bubbles; smooth the sides down firmly and trim.

Q. The etching process takes hours and the resulting glass is uneven and has milky patches.

A. The warmer the weather or room, the faster the etching process will be. If you want to speed up the process, pour some undiluted acid into the bath, a little at a time.

Q. My panel does not fit the window frame.

A. This situation should be avoided at all costs, however, if the problem has arisen these tips might be helpful: if the window is too big, first try to trim strips off the lead; if this does not work, take your panel back to the studio and cut the glass and lead up again without spoiling the design. If the window is too small, pack the recess with extra putty or silicon or add extra beading or pieces of lead. If the recess is too narrow, extend the frame by cutting four pieces of narrow metal beading to fit and slide them into the channels of the lead border. Alternatively, make a double lead border by sliding the lead came into the channel of the original lead border and solder it on. Neither solution is particularly elegant so it is preferable to cut the glass to fit.

Q. In a large fixed window, a piece of glass in the middle is broken. Do I need to take the whole window out of the frame?

A. No, you can repair it in situ if you are patient. First peel away the wings of the lead came around the piece on one side and push the broken piece out carefully. Replace the piece, push the wings back, apply some putty and then solder the corners.

Q. Where should I hang my free-hanging panel?

A. If your panel is quite dark, find a bright position, for instance a south-facing window, however if the panel is painted with great detail and subtlety, a north-facing window is ideal. If there is any frosting or sandblasting in the panel then a darker background, such as trees or houses, will bring out the subtle details.

5 A Gallery of Stained Glass

When I was attending a conference at the National Glass Centre in Sunderland, England in 1998, I met a very varied group of artists. Each had a distinctive style and had developed a personal approach to the art of stained glass. Some had explored new techniques, while others had concentrated on expressing a new language in glass. I will not attempt to categorize them, however they have all shown me how evocative and versatile a medium like glass can be in all its applications.

It is quite awe-inspiring how their work can be poetic, narrative and an invitation to look and wonder, all at the same time. Their inspiration comes from many sources: religion, intimate experiences, an emotional or rational response to a place, an object or a text, a joyful moment.

I hope you will find delight and inspiration in the following images and a few words supplied by the artist. Some are simple, small objects, whilst others are large, dramatic windows. Even if you cannot imagine producing more than a simple object at the moment, I hope this work will widen your view of the possibilities of glass and prove to be the beginning of a lifelong exploration into this medium.

RUTH TAYLOR JACOBSON, London

Witnesses (approximately 120cm × 95cm)

This triptych, inspired by carved wooden doors that once adorned an old synagogue in Kracow, is a memorial to the once vibrant Jewish communities of Eastern Europe. Traditional symbols – the Lion of Judah, the Eagle feeding her young, the Crown of Glory – are interspersed with verses from the Psalms,

Witnesses.

embodying the poetry, hope and despair of a shattered civilization. The figures on either side are the 'Witnesses': a Jew praying for his murdered people and a Polish woman selling yellow arm-bands.

Chanuka.

Chanuka (71cm × 43cm)

This 'Festival of Lights' commemorates the victory of the Maccabees over the Seleucid Greeks who tried to destroy Jewish religion. When the Temple in Jerusalem was re-captured, a small vial of pure oil was found, enough to light the Candelabrum for one day; but it lasted for eight days until new supplies were found. We light candles, adding one every night until all eight are ablaze. My image shows a candelabrum rising from dark blue to clear blue light. On its golden branches are the fruits of the land, and images of Joy and Hope found on ancient carvings.

RUTH KERSLEY GREISMAN, London

Garden, Private, London (137cm × 68.5cm)

This is a conservatory window overlooking a garden. The inspiration comes from underground plant and animal life, microscopic forms floating against a clear background through which glimpses of the real garden are seen. The colour was inspired by fields of rape, mustard and poppy on a summer evening in the Chilterns. I have acid-etched both flashed and un-flashed glass, on which the deep-etched relief has been painted. The black lines are made fluid by using the slow-drying clove oil. String leads have been stretched and curved over the panel's surface to create an ambiguity between the lead line and the painted line.

Birdman IV (The Automaton) (140cm × 36cm)

My initial sources were the bird-headed people from a 13th-century Passover

Haggadah, and later I was inspired by Egyptian mythology and Inuit art. Bird faces reflect our vulnerability and our aloneness; they speak of separation and isolation. This work also expresses the beauty of machinery, the icon of metropolis and the modern phenomenon of transforming the night sky by neon lighting.

This sculpture is free-standing and is an assemblage of both bird and robotic elements. Much of the glass has been

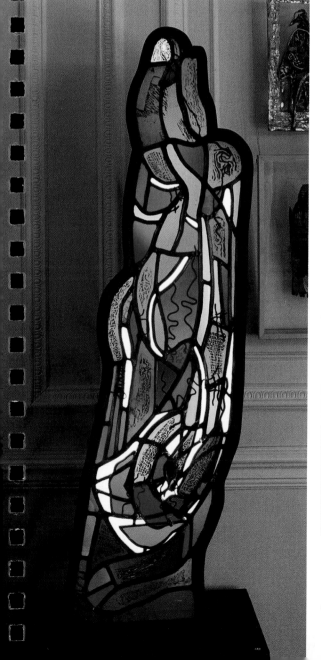

(Left) *Birdman IV.*   (Above) *Garden.*

acid-etched with paint forced into the deep grooves and then wiped off. String leads have been used as an extension of the painted line. The wing has been constructed to project from the flat body, and at the top within the head area is set the filament of a real light bulb.

Mater Private Hospital.

MARY MACKEY, Bandon, Ireland

Untitled, Mater Private Hospital, Dublin

Made for the Chapel of Rest in a hospital, these windows were designed to imbue an intimate space with a sense of spiritual belonging and shared concern, giving a shelter for grief, memories and hope. In each window there is light and dark, day and night. The warm colours of sunrise and sunset are set against the deep blue of the moonlit night sky. The rectangular linear structure, with the colour and proportion in both sections reversed, is balanced by the horizontal movement of the landscape of mountains and fields.

The four panels are fitted into steel frames and suspended in front of existing glazing. The windows are etched, painted and leaded. As they overlook an underground car park they are artificially lit.

Pennine Perpendicular II (76cm × 25cm, Free Hanging)

The shape of this panel (one of two autonomous panels), is inspired by the windows in the weavers' homes in Haworth, Yorkshire. These Pennine Perpendicular windows were made to allow in maximum light while at the same time providing protection from the wild winds off the moors. The painting on these panels was influenced by the dramatic nature of the moors, and also by the simultaneous stillness and movement of the Ryonji Rock Garden in Kyoto, Japan. Each panel is cut from a single sheet of flashed glass, etched and painted against natural light, loading up with a wide, flat brush and swirling it on, letting it dry and working back into it. This meant repainting each

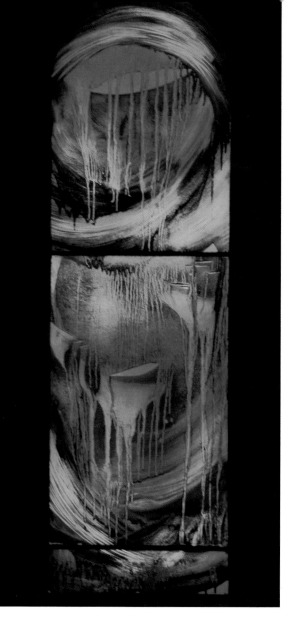

the first time since my teens. I enjoyed the ritual of lighting candles and saying my own prayers. I used pieces of coloured glass, which are painted with black tracing paint and fired. Holes are drilled into the glass and the pieces are wired together with metal wire.

(Left) *Pennine Perpendicular II.*

(Below) *'Wrap Him in Your Love'.*

panel several times before firing to achieve a unified sense of movement.

DONNA COOGAN, Cork, Ireland

'Wrap Him in Your Love' (36cm × 22.5cm)

The work that I make is mostly small in scale and of a personal nature. This work was made at a period in my life when I started to go to church again for

'His Heart was Unrepairable' (33cm × 31cm)

When a teenager, I lost my dad when he died during heart surgery. The text goes:

'He tried so hard to mend his heart. But in every place he tried to stitch his heart just fell apart'. I listened fascinated as my aunt told me this, she was a link to the doctor, to the last moments of my father's life. It gave me great comfort to visualize this caring doctor trying repeatedly to save him. His heart was unrepairable.

I used fused glass and black tracing paint and the pieces are wired together.

'His Heart Was Unrepairable'.

MARGARET CULLEN, Oxford

Fish and Chips (27cm × 21cm)

I saw a crumpled fish and chip paper in the street with pale shadows and straight creases and from this I designed this panel, adding a tropical fish – a clown trigger.

The chip paper is painted with a watered-down black oxide and the chips are painted in silver stain, both drawn into when dry with a sharp wooden point. The fish is blue flashed, engraved and painted with silver stain. The whole panel is leaded up, the outline resembling the shape of the crumpled chip paper.

JULIE HURST, Freeland, Oxfordshire

Holy City Panel (24cm × 24cm × 3cm)

This panel was inspired by St John's vision of the Holy City in Revelation 21. Agate slices and glass nuggets were copper-foiled in panels indicating the bejewelled foundations and twelve gates of pearl. These were leaded into textured clear and amber glass. The two panels were joined by bevels and the whole finished with decorative solder.

Fish and Chips.

Holy City panel.

ANITA PATE, East Lothian, Scotland

Detail from Music Room Window (Two Panels, 100cm × 35cm each)

(Below) *Music room window.*

(Below right) *Bathroom window.*

A house on the shore. The piping of the oystercatchers in the garden suggested the theme for this music room. Sandblasted plate using latex for textures.

Bathroom Window (135cm × 65cm)

Diving, one is suspended like my images at odd tangents – suspended while viewing the reflected glint of surface light through fronds of kelp. Floating pictures caught in time. Plated, streaky, antique, sandblasted.

LAURA JOHNSTON,
Newcastle upon Tyne

'Reflective Transmission', Window for Sunderland's Business and Innovation Centre

This window celebrates the history of glass making in the area. Antique hand-made glass, machine-made and 'high-tech' coated glasses all appear, providing a visual history. Dichroic glass (coated glass which reflects the light in dramatically changing colours at different angles) adds colour detail and two CDs, positioned towards the top of the window, refer to the role of glass in modern communications.

'Reflective Transmission' with detail (above).

'Shoal', National Glass Centre

Pieces of dichroic glass, 80m long, are suspended from the glass roof and sunlight is reflected and transmitted, animating the interior of the building with a spectrum of colours. The fluid form refers to the fascinating liquid/solid properties of glass and the work aims to portray the exciting nature of this material.

JANE McDONALD, Dorchester-on-Thames, Oxfordshire

Detail of Screen Panel (one of Two Panels, 125cm × 50cm)

The panels were inspired by Lyre birds seen in the Natural History Museum. Exterior banding in silver stain, interior colouring metallic lustres.

(Opposite above) *'Shoal'*,
National Glass Centre.

(Opposite below) *Detail of a
screen panel.*

Barbican screen.

Barbican Screen, 8 mil Etched Rear Panel (100cm × 75cm) with a 6 mil Painted Panel in Lustres and Silverstain (65cm Wide)

The design was inspired by Korean kimonos which were displayed in the Ashmolean Museum, Oxford.

My work has involved the development of new techniques for working with sheets of toughened or laminated glass, enabling large areas to be spanned without having to rely on traditional methods of assembly. Working with colour is undertaken by firing using flashed glass or putting metallic oxides (lustres) onto

the glass during the toughening process, making possible a wide variety of colour and imagery. Sandblasting and acid-etching can be used in conjunction with the lustres and flashed glass where colour is inappropriate and a lighter, more transparent surface is required.

MARTIN DONLIN, Dorset, England

Enamelled Glass Wall, Harbour Lights Cinema, Southampton

The background to the glass design is made up of two large blue forms based loosely on a 35mm and a 70mm film frame. The movement of film through the projector inspired the main shapes. The sandblasted forms, which become more prominent at night, correspond with the curve of the roof structure. The rhythmical composition of the various shapes were abstracted from a film leader. The design concentrates on a large area of colour in the centre with the intensity of the design fading towards one corner of the foyer to allow a view of the marina.

The 12mm toughened glass has been sandblasted and silk screen enamelled; the enamels are fired into the surface of the glass during the toughening process. I have applied a variety of images and textures by hand at various stages of the decorating process.

Tib Street Bridge Link, Smithfield Buildings, Manchester, England

The design is based upon a number of images of birds in flight. These images

have been abstracted, cut-up and layered as a collage. I have used earth colours and warm tones influenced by the surrounding buildings and brickwork. A circular form taken from a bird's eye view has been juxtaposed with a number of decorative forms intended to complement and enliven the design. The five icons in the squares are a reference to architectural details on the surrounding buildings, and a layout of Tib Street runs the full length of the design. A floor plan of part of the Smithfield Building is overlapped with a historic map of the northern quarter. I have also included a poem, referring to the Roman hero Horatius, who saved Rome from the Etruscans by single-handedly fighting them off while his fellow soldiers demolished the bridge behind him.

(Opposite) *An enamelled glass wall.*

(Above) *Tib Street Bridge link, Manchester.*

Useful Addresses

A list of glass societies and general stained glass suppliers

GLASS SOCIETIES

The British Society of Master Glass Painters
6, Queen Square
London WC1N 3AR
UK

Contemporary Glass Society
PO Box 1320
Stoke on Trent ST4 2YF
UK

Stained Glass Association of America
6 SW Second Street, Suite 7
Lee's Summit
MO 64063
USA

International Glass Guild of America
54 Cherry Street
PO Box 1809
North Adams
MA 01247-1809
USA

The Western Australian Art Glass Guild Incorporated
PO Box 288
North Fremantle
WA 6159
Australia

Glass Craft Australia
12–14 Ceylon Street
Nunawading
Victoria 3131
Australia

GENERAL STAINED GLASS SUPPLIERS

Europe

James Hetley & Co. Limited
Glasshouse Fields
London E1 9JA
UK

Lead & Light
Coloured Glass Warehouse/Workshop
35a Hartland Road
London NW1 4BD
UK

Pearsons Glass Limited
65 James Watt Place
College Milton
East Kilbride G74 5HG
Scotland, UK

Kansa Craft
The Flour Mill
Wath Road
Elsecar
Barnsley S74 8HW
UK

Dublin Stained Glass Supplies
62b Heather Road
Sandy Ford Industrial Estate
Dublin 18
County Dublin
Ireland

Leonard Tiffany Import-Export
30, Hoveniersstraat
B 2018 Antwerp
Belgium

Glass Heiliger
Im Mullenfeld 29
Bonn 53123
Germany

Atelier S
Bassac
Chateauneuf-sur-Charente 16120
France

Studio Lood om oud Glas
Binnen Oranjestraat 17
Amsterdam HZ-1013
Netherlands

Joern B. Olsen
Klosterstraede 21
Copenhagen 1157
Denmark

Video-Comm Bt Laszlo Gyorbiro
Vizeses U. 13
Budapest Arapadfald 1164
Hungary

Fantasy Craft Sas Di M. Di Spirito & C.
Via Desiderio 3/9
Milano 20131
Italy

Stained Glass
Lourou 4
Patra 26442
Greece

Atelier Tiffany-Time
Rue De L'Horloge
Lutry 1095
Switzerland

Vidrio Y Luz
Butron, 2-3 A
Madrid 28022
Spain

USA

Albert Stained Glass
57 Front Street
Brooklyn
NY 11201

S.A. Bendheim Company Inc.
61, Willett Street
Passaic
NJ 07055

Delphi Stained Glass
3380 Jolly Road
Lansing
MI 48910

Hollander Glass Central Inc.
1505 Centre Circle
Downers Grove
Chicago
IL 60515

Fransiscan Glass Company Inc.
100 San Antonio Circle
Mountain View
CA 94040

Houston Stained Glass Supply
2002 Brittmoore Street
Houston
TX 77043

Northwest Art Glass
9003 151st Avenue NE
Redmond
WA 98052

Canada

Monarch Stained Glass
49, Chatham Street South
Blenheim
Ontario N0P 1A0

Kaleido Glass Ltd
2, Lamb Street
Georgetown
Ontario L7G 3M9

Australia

The Stained Glass Professionals
83, Lysaght Street
Mitchell
Australian Capital Territory 2911

Bob Bush Leadlights
102, Smith Street
Summer Hill
New South Wales 2130

Seale Stained Glass
528, White House Road
Surrey Hills
Victoria 3127

New Zealand

Debsglass
51, Bell Road
Gracefield
Lower Hutt
Wellington 064

Sauvarins Coloured Glass Merchants
474 New North Roads
Kingsland
Auckland

Index